VICTORIAN GARDENS

VICTORIAN GARDENS

John Highstone

Plant Drawings by Kevin Haapala
Landscape Plan Drawings by Carol Carlson

1817

HARPER & ROW, PUBLISHERS, SAN FRANCISCO

Cambridge, Hagerstown, New York, Philadelphia
London, Mexico City, São Paulo, Sydney

Photos on pages 4 (bottom), 7, 14 (top and bottom),
18, 28, 31, and 67 are reproduced from *Gardens for
Small Country Houses* by Gertrude Jekyll and
Sir Lawrence Weaver (London: Country Life
Ltd., 1912).

FIRST EDITION

Designed by Donna Davis

Library of Congress Cataloging in Publication Data

Victorian gardens.

Bibliography: p. 173
Includes index.
1. Gardens, Victorian. I. Haapala, Kevin.
II. Carlson, Carol. III. Title.
SB458.7.K7 1980   635.9   80-8342
ISBN 0-06-250481-9   ·

---

82 83 84 85 86 10 9 8 7 6 5 4 3 2 1

CONTENTS

I.

A BACKWARD GLANCE

The Victorian era brought with it more than a change in social mores; it also heralded a new concept in gardening. The Industrial Revolution meant a great increase in population, especially in urban areas, and an emergent wealthy class distinct in background from the landowners who created the great English gardens.

ENGLISH LANDSCAPE ARCHITECTS

Humphrey Repton (1752–1818) was perhaps a better salesman than he was a landscape architect, but he was a sensitive man with an eye for beauty. He was not qualified as a botanist or a landscape gardener, but he recognized new trends and new social movements, and knew that, because of the Industrial Revolution and its resulting migration of people to places of their own, gardens would be in demand. In his *Enquiry into the Changes of Taste in Landscape Gardening* (1806), Repton stated his four principles of landscape gardening: (1) the garden should display natural beauty but hide natural defects; (2) the garden should give the appearance of freedom by disguising or hiding boundaries; (3) the garden should carefully conceal every interference of art, making the whole look as if it were totally produced by nature; and (4) the garden should have no objects of mere convenience or comfort. These principles went against the views of the great Lancelot "Capability" Brown, then-reigning horticultural planner.

Brown operated on a grand scale; his garden work, it was said—or he said—was done with a poet's feeling and a painter's eye. (In the early 1800s, poetry, painting, and gardening were regarded as related arts.) Lancelot Brown was the master garden artist. Under his influence, grand parklike gardens abounded, and lakes and hills were incorporated into his vast "paintings." Contours of green turf, mirrors of still water, and a few species of trees used singly or in belts were the standard of the day. In the *Rise and Progress of the Present Taste* (1767), it was said,

> Born to grace Nature, and her works complete;
> With all that's beautiful, sublime and great!
> For him each Muse enwreathes the Laurel Crown,
> And consecrates to Fame immortal Brown.

Repton's contribution was to take the idea of a garden as a park or huge estate and miniaturize it, making it every person's own floral and foliage display.

John Claudius Loudon, a Scot, recognized the significance of the changing style and refined it. Unlike Repton, who had been in commerce before his advent on the garden scene, Loudon was a designer, nurseryman, writer, botanist and architect. With his wife, he published the *Suburban Gardener* (1838), for many years the bible of the new and rapidly rising middle class. Loudon merged the growing interest in horticulture with the art of making a smaller natural scene. As a result the garden, no longer the exclusive domain of a privileged few, became the delight of the middle class. The flowering gardens dotting present-day London and its suburbs owe a great deal to this one man.

Loudon's notions on landscape gardening are summed up in his own *Arboreteum et Fruticetum Britannicum* (1838):

> A residence laid out in the modern manner with the surface of the ground disposed in imitation of the undulations of nature, and the trees scattered over it in groups and masses, neither in straight lines, nor cut into artificial shapes, might be mistaken for nature, were not the trees planted chiefly of foreign kinds not to be met with in the natural or general scenery of the country. Everything in modern landscape gardening, therefore, depends on the use of foreign trees and shrubs; and, when it is once properly understood that no residence in the modern style can have a claim to be considered as having been laid out in good taste, on

A public garden? No, this vast formal garden of Victorian flavor is from a private residence. The symmetrical plan (with pairs of plants) shows the lingering influence of "Capability" Brown. The overall effect is quite handsome. (Photo by Matthew Barr.)

When vast acreage is available, it is possible to extend a lawn into infinity and create a painting-like quality — pretty to view but almost impossible to have these days. The plant material is beautifully placed here: one monumental tree and three groups of plants to balance the scene. (Photo by Matthew Barr.)

This garden typifies the Victorian look: the lawn is a green canvas, the shrubs are appropriately placed for mass and dimension, and the incredible array of walls, levels, and steps all combine to create a pleasing scene. The house is off in the distance.

which all the trees and shrubs employed are not either foreign ones, or improved varieties of indigenous ones, the grounds of every country seat from the cottage to the mansion will become an arboretum, differing only in the number of species which it contains.

Although Loudon led this transition, the gardening history of the nineteenth century was a melting pot of different views, reflecting those of society itself. Victorian England was a middle-class society, and if there was a truly collective vision among the Victorians, it was harbored by the middle class rather than the aristocracy.

THE VICTORIAN STYLE

The Victorian or Repton style provided for a garden of seclusion and natural beauty, a created segment of nature. The planned unity of the formal garden was demolished by Repton—no more axial development (one plant on each side, one tree on each side), no more sweeping walks. Now a garden included, as an integral part of the plan, lawn, shrubbery (including the exotics, which had previously been frowned on), a terrace walk, and a conservatory. Let us explore these concepts more carefully, because they are clues to the good Victorian garden—and they make sense.

Without doubt, a luxurious green carpet of grass enhances any garden—it makes it appear lush and attuned to nature. Even a small lawn creates this effect. In addition, flower beds, trees, and shrubs seem more natural in combination with lawns, which contribute to the cohesiveness of the garden.

Shrubbery and flowering plants in general came into vogue in the Victorian garden; people began to recognize the beauty and wonder of nature and wanted a closer union with it. They wanted not only to have plants, but to see and enjoy them, and for the first time in history the average person could actually afford to do so.

Repton retained one element from the grand gardens, the terrace walk, incorporating it into the more intimate house gardens. The terrace walk (or balustrade or parterre) was generally a paved area between the house and the garden beyond. It was a necessary link, a transitional element that prepared one for the lawn area and garden. The Victorians had started to enjoy nature, it is true, and they wanted closer contact with plants, but they still wanted some remnant of separation between themselves and the unknown. The terrace provided this.

As the Victorian period continued, the appreciation of plants and flowers also flourished. People wanted to have growing things inside as well as outside, and thus the conservatory became very popular. Also, and most importantly, middle-class people could now afford glass. Generally the greenhouse was outside the home, but solariums (indoor greenhouses) were also added to many homes. In addition to the greenhouse, other decorative features were used in gardens. Cast iron was fashionable; many sorts of garden constructions, especially trellises, were made of the material.

Trelliage was immensely popular. Repton claimed to have reintroduced this gardening element, and he used wood as well as cast iron. Trelliage does for a garden what icing does for a cake: it makes it.

Statues and urns took their place in the garden as naturally as trees and shrubs. In this Victorian blending of man and nature, one feature of the earlier grand manner of gardening was retained.

Cast-iron fences and gates also were part of the Victorian garden because they were pretty and added to the gingerbread effect. They make the same statement in a garden today and are handsome even when copied in wood or other materials.

Beds devoted to specific plants were typical of this gardening period. These beds took many shapes, from elaborate fern leaves to fleur-de-lis. If the forerunners of Victorian gardeners could make patterns on the ground with colored sand and boxwood, why not similar patterns made with alyssum and lobelia and geraniums?

As Repton evolved his style of garden, he took into consideration an important aspect of gardening and planning: the house and garden should match each other. A house should be to its garden as a bonsai plant is to its container. They should complement each other, not compete. The Victorian home, with its elaborate art and gingerbread decorations, required a garden of similar composition, one that was decorative and picturesque.

The shrubbery and flowers of a Victorian garden did in fact complement the decorativeness of the home and lawn, creating the proper marriage. Before Repton's time, the cutting garden or flower area was always hidden from the house. Now it came into its own as part of the garden, and meandering paths added to the charm.

Today, in most cities, the Victorian house occupies a long, narrow lot, and thus the garden must become an extension of this already existing site. Properly landscaped with suitable shrubs, trees, and flowers, the long, narrow lot works well as a unifier, letting the garden and the house complement each other.

Although the styles have been modified, the principles of Victorian gardens remain. The garden has become a place for people rather than a vast landscape for solitary viewing—a place where one can both appreciate and participate in beauty. When the gardener entered the garden, the land-

Flowers have finally made their appearance en masse in this scene from an English country garden of about 1900. Although there is still an expanse of green (not in the picture), the grouping of flowers now tends to bring nature closer to the house. Note how the character of the garden is in union with that of the house. The result is a congenial, cottage-like effect.

This garden, one of many gardens on an estate, is Victorian in style. The design is basically symmetrical, and flowers are absent. Shrubs and trees are the garden, with an interesting array of graceful paths. (Photo by Scharmer.)

A Victorian garden beautifully recreated today incorporates the lawn, flower beds, shrubs, and trees beyond. The grandiose feeling is gone: the Victorian elements are all here, but in compact design. (Photo by Molly Adams.)

scape painting style that typified vast gardens disappeared. It has never resurfaced, largely because of today's limited space for gardens. Thus Repton's garden is now *everyone's* garden.

THE NINETEENTH-CENTURY GARDEN IN AMERICA

There were really no professional garden landscapers in America until the nineteenth century. The influence of Andrew Parmentier was great, but it was A. J. Downing, a member of a family of nurserymen and a voluminous writer, who first established garden design in the English style in America. Like Loudon, he had a keen eye for design and a boundless interest in horticulture. Before Downing, little thought had been given to gardens either for public use or private enjoyment in America. It is true that William Penn laid out Philadelphia as a garden city in the late seventeenth century, but he did so for an eminently practical reason: he wanted to ensure there would be no repetition in his town of the Great Fire of London.

While studying gardening in England, Downing met Calvert Vaux and persuaded him to come to the United States as his business partner. It was through Downing's influence, particularly his writings, that New York City began to lay plans in 1858 for Central Park. Thus it seems only just that after Downing's death, it was Vaux, teamed with Frederick Law Olmsted, who won the contract for planning Central Park. Engineer, farmer, and agricultural journalist, Olmsted in time became the best-known landscape gardener in America.

There is scant information available about the small private gardens of America. We do know, however, that for the most part ornamental gardens were few in number. Because Americans needed produce, householders concentrated on fruit and kitchen gardens. Except in the deep South, where flowers were grown extensively, the era of the purely ornamental American garden was still some decades away; the great boom of flower growing taking place in England did not cross the ocean for some time.

2.

PLANTING ARRANGEMENTS

The suggested planting layouts and arrangements in this book are based on Victorian concepts, somewhat updated. Generally, however, the old principles are valid. The suggestions can be modified to your specific grounds; they serve as a starting point. What follow are the seven basic premises of the Victorian garden plan, discussed in detail in the rest of the chapter.

1. Install in one or more places a space of unbroken lawn. The space is determined by the size and shape of the site.
2. Plant from the house itself to the lot lines, leaving views and vistas.
3. Plant the largest trees and shrubs away from the lawn area.
4. On small sites, limit trees to just a few, concentrating instead on shrubs and flowers.
5. Keep plant groups together; that is, plant trees and shrubs in one area rather than scattering them throughout the site.
6. Insist on convenience: if there is a kitchen or vegetable garden, make it convenient to the house.
7. Install graceful paths and walks.

UNBROKEN LAWN (Premise 1)

The garden with a lawn is always more intimate, more charming, and more beautiful than the landscape without a green carpet, because a lawn is natural and brings into the small garden the illusion of a larger park. The lawn need not be large. For example, my own small garden in Napa, California, is fashioned after a Victorian plan. The area outside the bedroom—the last room in the house—looks onto a small hillside and then beyond to open space. I am fond of flowers and wanted color, but I realized that a mass of color would be jarring in relation to the great outdoor landscape beyond. I made a lawn area of only 15 by 20 feet curving into a valley. This lawn is difficult to maintain but worth the effort because of the effect. Small trees were cleared away to make an unbroken expanse of green. When the lawn grew, I had what I wanted: a green canvas for the deeper green trees beyond. This worked well, but something was still missing: flowers. So, at the edge of the lawn I planted a small border—about 8 feet wide—of perennials and annuals in a graceful curve, with a few shrubs beyond. I thus attained an intimate look, and the added flower color neither detracted from nor clashed with the look of the whole garden. The flowers added the necessary unity. The existing trees and shrubbery make my lawn look bigger than it is.

OPEN VISTA (Premise 2)

If you plant in lines radiating from the house to the outside margin of the lot, you create pleasant views from the house. Again, let me use my small Victorian garden as an example. The 50-foot-long, 30-foot-wide view from the front of the house opens onto hills and valleys full of ancient trees and falls away to a deeper valley. I wanted to keep this vista open, yet some planting was necessary to create a visual bridge from the house to the distant hills. If I left the area bare, it would look just that: barren. What was needed was plant material that would correlate the house and the land with the great beyond.

My gardening plan included small shrubs planted in arcs in two locations: the first near the left side of the house, which is the entrance, the second somewhat in back of the first group. Beyond these two groups of shrubs, a vertical accent was needed to tie into the natural accent of trees beyond. I planted a small beech tree in one area and two mimosa trees next to each other in another area nearby. The view was deliberately left open in the center. I next planted a strip of lawn about 15 feet wide. But then the right side of the house was not balanced. I did not want to create a formal

This seaside garden shows an uninterrupted expanse of lawn bordered by flower beds. The symmetry, very much a note from the past, is again evident. (Photo by Roche.)

The vista from the house was important in Victorian days. This photo shows a typically park-like setting, with vast acreage beyond.

Beyond the flower garden and bordered by a geometrical hedge in the distance are the trees. This feature was a popular and established premise of Victorian gardening.

symmetrical plan, with shrubs and trees duplicated on either side, so I "stretched" the lawn area from the adjacent bedroom area so that it swung around the house and planted one small beech tree near this lawn area.

You may think that the beech tree breaks Premise 1, but it really does not, because the lawn expanse adjacent to the bedroom remains unbroken. The one tree around the corner of the house helps esthetically to anchor the house in place. Thus my planting was minimal, yet the two groups of shrubs, three trees to the left and one tree to the right, accomplished the picture I wanted.

PLACEMENT OF SHRUBS AND TREES (Premise 3)

Beyond the main vista of my Napa property, ancient trees and shrubs grow luxuriously. I thus had a beautiful present from nature to work with. The shrubs and several trees planted at the front of the house, when viewed against the grand scale of this natural landscape, make the whole lawn area look larger. This strip of lawn, extending to the front of the house, uses the Victorian concept of a terrace or parterre and coordinates the house site to the site beyond.

If you do not have a natural gift of a distant forest or valley, plant your own trees and shrubs to create a vista. Use nature's principle: plant the biggest trees and shrubs far away from the lawn area, to create a frame. But be sure you do not block your view; keep some areas open, as explained in Premise 2. Remember, you want to be able to look out on nature and at the same time have nature look in at you.

PLANTING SMALL SITES (Premise 4)

Planting small gardens can be challenging but rewarding. A small garden site is about all that is available in cities, yet lack of room need not prevent you from having a Victorian garden. I will prove this point by discussing what I did with the postage-stamp lot I had when I first moved to San Francisco in 1961. I rented an apartment that was part of an authentic Victorian house, and because the other tenants were not interested in landscaping and the lot was literally a mess, I decided to plant a garden.

The house had been built in 1890 and was wonderfully restored—complete with portico—by my landlord, the owner. The house still stands—as does the garden, just the way I planted it. The original lot was 25 feet wide by 100 feet long, but through convoluted variances, the garden, or part of it, had been sold with another house across the way. As a result, the lot when I first saw it in 1961 was only 25 feet wide and approximately 35 feet long.

Small sites can have Victorian flavor too. This postage stamp garden, a pleasant place to sit and think, is quite charming; flowers are few and shrubs predominate. (Photo by Scharmer.)

The "lawn," a weedy path in disrepair, was framed by a wooden fence, and there were some remnants of shrubbery as well as one old oak tree that completely robbed the garden of sun and space.

First I had the tree removed and the ground turned. Then I was ready to develop a garden plan. I came up with a small lawn of unbroken expanse—as far as that was possible—along with the adroit placement of flowers, shrubs, and a small tree. Shrubbery was planted in graceful curves to the right—in a concentrated grouping—and at the rear low-growing shrubs with a flower border around the lawn. To the left were even smaller shrubs and vines and one well-selected tree. I replaced the fence with a new wooden one that was embellished with some trelliswork. A small arbor at the front of the garden tied the plan together.

Two curved paths were installed and circled the garden. Much trimming and pruning were necessary through the years, but the garden today complements the house, and the house blends with the garden. Six of the principles of Victorian design were used throughout. No vista was possible because of the limited space and closeness of the property to other homes. The best I could do was to open up the center of the lot to the adjoining property and hope for the best.

GROUPING PLANTS (Premise 5)

Plant your trees, shrubs, and flowers in matched groups. Several shrubs of one kind will create a mass, but a single shrub looks out of place. The larger your property, the more groups you can have. You can vary the species somewhat—such as rhododendron in one area, camellias in another—but keep the grouping in mind, because it makes a world of difference. If at all possible, repeat the group somewhere else on the property. And always avoid dead-center placement; shrubs and trees should be used to frame or create vistas, not obstruct them.

Try to use any existing large trees. If you have just one large tree, which might be overbearing, plant a few related trees nearby to fill out the space. In time the trees will grow into a cohesive group concept, and the whole area will be pleasing to look at. (Although one large tree can be overbearing, one really *distinctive* tree can be a dramatic accent to a smaller site rather than an isolated exclamation point, as in a large lot.) Do not balance one tree to the left of the house with one tree to the right of the house. Plant three or five trees on one side, and then repeat this arrangement midway in the landscape plan. Repeat such a grouping a third or fourth time if the site is larger. Keep the trees away from the garden proper; follow Premise 3 in having large trees and shrubs in the distance.

17

In the old English garden, plants are grouped, never single, and thus create a full effect framed by evergreen shrubs. All is in keeping with the house.

Plant flower beds the same way. Have a concentration of color and repeat it asymmetrically elsewhere on the property to retain balance and proportion. I prefer flowers in drifts (groups), as a frame around the lawn rather than actually in the lawn area.

CONVENIENCE (Premise 6)

If you are fortunate enough to have space for a greenhouse or vegetable garden, locate it near the house and plan it as an integral part of the garden. The vegetable garden, which can include flowers for cutting, can be very charming when adjacent to the kitchen.

Use a small area for a kitchen garden, because a large expanse of vegetables or flowers is not necessary. A good size is 10 by 20 feet; you can

This array of color in lovely flower beds is a mass grouping of plants that works well. Tall trees and shrubs provide the background. (Photo by Molly Adams.)

Come walk the garden path amidst flowers and green — a pleasant place to stroll. (Photo by author.)

grow almost anything in a space that size. Be sure the spot gets sun because vegetables and flowers must have a great deal of sun to prosper. If at first the vegetable garden looks isolated or out of place, judiciously plant flower beds or hedges and connect this garden to the main garden by installing a graceful walk.

The greenhouse also should be an adjunct to the house. A lean-to greenhouse is a perfect way to do this, and it will increase the value of your property. I believe that my previous house sold only because of its lovely garden room, which opened to the garden proper, providing an extension of the outdoors indoors.

PATHS AND WALKS (Premise 7)

This important aspect of garden landscaping is too often neglected. A garden is a place for solace and relaxation, but if you cannot walk your property to enjoy it, let alone to tend it, it can be a chore.

Install curving and graceful walks; straight walks are invariably uninteresting. The paths should be an integral part of the garden plan, following the garden lines rather than looking like tacked-on afterthoughts.

The materials for walks can be brick, gravel, or any other paving material. Make the walks wide enough for two people to walk side by side. And, to follow Premise 1, do not put a path or walk between or into a garden lawn area. Leave the lawn unbroken, with the paths soothingly meandering among the trees, shrubs, and flower beds.

3.

GARDEN PLANNING

We now have the premises of the Victorian garden plan. In addition, it is prudent to know something about general garden design. This is approached on three levels: scale, proportion, and unity. Then, as now, these are the elements of a good garden.

You should also know how to plan on paper—which is not as difficult as it sounds. It means making sketches of the garden design on paper before you start any planning or rejuvenation of an existing site.

Consider all aspects of the situation before you start laying out the garden plan on paper. Use your feet as well as your head: walk the property several times, look at the house from the grounds, and then view the property from inside the house.

SCALE, PROPORTION, AND UNITY

Plants have definite shapes and forms: spreading, horizontal, vertical, round, weeping, or trailing. For example, dogwood, pin oak, and hawthorn have strong horizontal lines that carry the eye from one plant to another. These are good selections for low, flat houses. Beech, flowering cherry, or

Scale, proportion, and unity are well shown in this garden; there is a perfect marriage of trees, shrubs, flowers, and lawns. The varying heights, mass, and volume are all well proportioned. (Photo by Molly Adams.)

weeping willow are delicate and fragile in appearance, create soft lines, and are good in front of stiffer subjects.

The form of a plant is vitally important in landscaping, but unless you know what a plant will look like when it is mature, selecting seeds or little plants is something of a guessing game. When you make your plant selections, try to visualize the plant fully grown. Some species lose their symmetrical form with age. Others, such as pines and some of the firs, lose their lower branches as they get older.

Scale and proportion must be carefully considered in landscaping, because they are the keys to an attractive setting. Scale is the graduated visual relationship of each plant's form to every other plant's form and to the garden design as a whole. A large house looks incongruous with a small entrance; a cottage with an elaborate court and garden is unpleasing. You must establish an appealing scale between the garden and the house. The starting point can be a tree. A large tree will link the house and the garden.

All the elements of a Victorian garden are brought together in this charming garden: trees and shrubs in the background, an uninterrupted expanse of lawn, and (closer to the house and defined by a beautiful iron fence) the charming flower borders and formal shrub design. (Photo by Hedrich Blessing.)

With a small house, the usual procedure is to have a small tree, but here the principle can be altered: use a very large tree to make the house seem charming.

Proportion is the harmonious relationship of one part of a total picture to another and to the whole. It is balance or symmetry. A large, paved terrace should be balanced with a small lawn, a small patio with a large lawn. To make both areas the same size is a mistake, because then there is no interest; one element does not complement the other. Vertical forms should be balanced with several horizontal elements.

Unity is harmony, the successful blending of plants to create a whole garden. You do not want a hodgepodge of unrelated masses insulting the eye. Plants of related forms, colors, and textures achieve the unity every attractive garden needs.

Another element to consider is rhythm, which is repeating the same group of plants or the same plant to give a sense of movement.

If you think about each term—*scale, proportion,* and *unity*—you will realize that each one depends on the others; they are all interrelated. Generally, if you get the scale and proportion right, unity and rhythm fall in line. The following planning rules should help.

1. Accentuate the vertical and horizontal lines of the home with appropriate plantings of trees and shrubs.
2. Use well-designed plant groups at the corners of the home to soften any strong architectural lines and to give more width to the house if necessary.
3. Remember that well-groomed specimen plants are always assets.
4. Make the planting area pleasing in shape. For example, straight, single rows of plants are tiresome to the eye, but flowing curves and free-form patterns provide dramatic interest.
5. Use vines to soften fences and create vertical swaths of color.
6. Use ground cover and edging material where necessary.
7. Provide horizontal accent with low-growing evergreens, such as yews and junipers, hollies and barberries.

PLANNING ON PAPER

The idea of planning your garden on paper may seem silly, but it is much easier to erase a pencil mark than to demolish a fence or pull out a tree.

A general ground plan for the garden site does not have to be drawn to scale; at first, it can be just a sketch. If possible, get a plot plan of the house (which shows the dimensions of the site) from your builder. If you are the second or third owner of a place, measure your property and make a plot

The beauty of a well-landscaped garden is evident here. The large, mature trees flank the house, there is an area of lawn, and in the foreground lies a fine, old-fashioned flower garden. (Photo by Molly Adams.)

The Victorian gardening premises are evident in this charming small side yard. The flower beds are close to the house, and a lovely archway in the rear opens on a lawn and, beyond, on shrubs and trees.

plan. Next, using your plan as a guide, transpose the property's boundary lines onto graph paper. Let each square represent 1 foot. Now draw in, to scale, the outline of the house, and include steps, walks, driveways, and existing trees and shrubs.

Determine the ground slope, because this can make a difference in a plan. Stretch a string crossways across the plot. Using a mason's level, measure the distance between the ground and the string to determine just how much grade there is. Note the high and low areas and how much the grade drops; mark these measurements on the graph paper. Now put in the designations that show where there is sun and shade and where the north point is. Study the composition. If all the existing features are present on the graph, you can really start planning the garden now.

Over the graph paper, lay a sheet of tracing paper. Nearby, keep a previously made list of what you want in the garden and the areas for a patio, play space, and service area. First sketch the traffic patterns on the tracing paper. Then draw in the rough sizes and shapes of objects you want outdoors, such as terrace, flower beds, raised beds, new trees and shrubs, pools or fountains, and whatever else is necessary to your overall plan. The irregular shapes you have drawn should start to relate to each other. Shade them in to see if you are achieving balance and proportion. If you are not pleased with the layout—and first arrangements are rarely satisfactory—start over on a new piece of tracing paper. Consider all things carefully, and make several plans so that all members of the family have a chance to contribute.

Once you have a rough sketch agreeable to all, do a detailed design. This time, use colored pencils to shade in the negative areas, to get an effect of the planned color combination. Exactness counts now, so be sure to have proper measurements of the house and lot, objects, and existing plant material. This is the time to decide how much construction will be necessary in the garden—fences, terraces, pools, walls—and how much planting will be needed. Here are some ideas to help you plan.

Rectangular or square patterns are simple and the most natural to use. They are usually projections of the house form. Working with a uniform module (that is, a space repeated again and again) simplifies a plan. The module can be 3 by 4 feet or 5 by 5 feet, or almost any size block that fits your needs. The patio can be paved with 3 by 4 blocks, stepping-stones can be the same size, and planting islands and beds can also relate to the same module. In this way, every design line in the plan is in proportion and pleasing to the eye, with simplicity and concise organization of space.

Acute or obtuse angles or triangles reflect the angular form of the house and site and lead the eye to a focal point, giving a sense of space and direction. Circular forms add interest to a pattern and, in proper balance with straight lines, can create a pleasing composition. Free curves are curving lines with a constantly changing radius. These are sweeping natural lines and, skillfully used with geometric forms, produce richness in motion.

PATHS AND WALKS

Paths and walks were very much part of the Victorian garden. As a new kinship with plants and flowers came into being, the idea of getting around the garden became vital; paths and walks were thus paramount. Victorians liked their evening strolls, and the garden was a retreat—a place to be alone with one's thoughts or together with a loved one, a place for people and for walking and enjoying nature at close view. Unfortunately, in most American gardens the paths and walks are all too often forgotten.

Lay out paths and walks in your original plans, and make them pleasing. By that I mean have graceful aisles that curve and arc. Curves and arcs do not make the garden formal; rather, they make the patterns of ingress and egress appealing to the eye. Straight paths are, of course, also feasible, especially if there is a garden feature such as a fountain or statue at the end, but they need more clever planning to be effective than do curved ones.

Be sure your paths give you full access to all of your grounds. Do not waste a secluded spot in back of the house because it is difficult to get to. (A secret garden with a path leading to it can be infinitely charming.) A path should not be used simply to get from one place to another, however; it should be a decorative feature as well—an attractive pattern to break the monotony of a large area or a finely detailed ornate path with colorful tile, for example.

CONSTRUCTION OF PATHS AND WALKS.   The construction of the path is important, too—its suitability to the site and use, its cost, and the question of its upkeep.

Paths should lead to a point of interest or connect with other paths. Make them broad enough—at least 3 to 5 feet wide—for two people to walk abreast. There is nothing more frustrating than a narrow path. The width should have some relation to the length; good proportion is important.

Brick is a popular material for paths because it harmonizes well with nearly every outdoor situation. It is easy to install and can simply be laid on a well-tamped-down sand or cinder base. It can be put down in many

The flowers are "as high as an elephant's eye" in this fine old English garden. There is truly a concentration of color, and adjoining shrubs and trees are a perfect foil for the panorama of beauty.

Combinations of masonry work well together; here concrete and fieldstone pavers complement each other. (Photo by Matthew Barr.)

patterns to add an interesting note to the garden, and it lasts for years.

Concrete is durable, but it is not always suitable because of its sterile gray color. It must be installed with a good foundation so that it is not cracked by frost. Concrete stepping-stones are decorative and easy to put in place; so are patio pavers and patio blocks. Investigate local building supply yards carefully because there are many new types of stepping-stones available.

Flagstone or gravel or grass paths are handsome, but flagstone is rarely inexpensive, and gravel has to be replaced frequently. And grass has limitations if there is heavy foot traffic. Before you make a final choice, determine the following:

- Will the paving have a pleasant feel underfoot?
- Will the color, pattern, and texture blend with other surfaces?
- Will it withstand weather?
- Will it last a long time?
- Will it be easy to clean?
- Will you be able to install it yourself?
- Will weeds grow through it?

Steps in the garden are necessary where there is a change of levels. They need not be merely functional, however; they can break the monotony of a landscape with graceful and sweeping lines to add visual interest to the plan. They do not have to be straight or precise unless you have a very formal garden.

A straight flight of steps is hardly pleasing; turns and angles with wide or low treads are more effective in the landscape. Generally, a 14-inch tread with a rise of about 6 inches is recommended.

If there is a long flight of steps, break it up with landings between, perhaps with a change of direction. There is a vast array of materials available for steps — concrete or pieces of brick, pre-cast slabs, logs or railroad ties, to mention a few.

As a rule, steps do not require perfect detailing, because plants can be used to soften the rough edges.

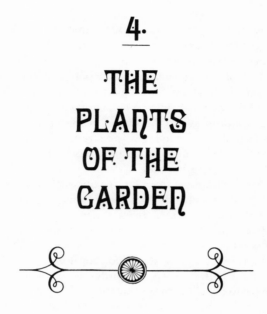

4.

THE
PLANTS
OF THE
GARDEN

In the Victorian era, imported exotic plants, shrubs, and trees were enormously popular in gardens. Plants never seen before became topics of great conversation, and to have them growing in one's garden was considered a coup, a status symbol. However, the proliferation of such new trees and shrubs could give the garden a restless, disorderly appearance. Repton recognized this hazard and advised that only a few sorts be mixed in any one given area. This practice, coupled with asymmetrical planting design, did for a time create gardens that, although they were hardly pleasing to view, were still considered grand because they had examples of the foreign imports.

TREES

Trees are the backbone of most gardens. However, it is quite possible to have a charming Victorian landscape without trees in the garden proper, as long as trees are on adjoining land. Trees vary in shape, from columnar to canopy, and in color; some are deciduous, losing leaves in winter, and others are evergreen, notably the conifers that are a rich green all year. There are trees for all kinds of situations and landscape plans.

The deciduous trees most often used in Victorian gardens of the past were oak, elm, ash, linden, acacia, beech, poplar, horse chestnut, birch, alder, maple, locust, mulberry, sweet gum, walnut, hickory, willow, catalpa, magnolia, and dogwood.They were almost exclusively ornamental—picturesque trees appropriate to the Victorian reference. The same species are all available today, often in improved strains.

Evergreens of the time included pine (perhaps the most common), spruce, cedar, yew, and arborvitae.

It is hard to recommend trees for specific regions of the country, because what you grow depends on where you live. There are ten climate zones within the United States; these zones are designated by the U.S. Department of Agriculture and are numbered according to their frost-hardiness. Most nurseries that sell trees, and all mail-order houses, list the zone a tree supposedly does best in. If you buy in your own locale, you need not worry about whether the tree is hardy—it will be. If you buy by mail order, you have to be a little more cautious.

Trees must be planted properly: deep in the ground, their roots well anchored in good, fresh topsoil for nutrition. In their first few years, trees require a good deal of water—if it does not rain, you must provide water—and some occasional feeding to get them going. Once established, however, trees generally take care of themselves if occasionally pruned and trimmed.

LIST OF TREES

Abies (fir).   Generally, abies or fir evergreens are pyramidal in shape and have rigid horizontal branches, making them a decisive accent in the landscape. Use them sparingly. Their needles stay on the trees for about five years before they fall; the cones are ornamental but do not appear every year. The trees have few insect or disease problems, but as they mature the lower branches become unsightly, and once removed they do not grow back, so a mature specimen lacks symmetry. Firs deteriorate rapidly in warm, dry climates. These trees are Christmas favorites.

Acacia.   Acacias are evergreen shrubs and trees suitable to temperate areas. They differ widely in foliage and growth habit: some have feathery, divided leaves, and others have flattened leaves. Acacias are short-lived (to about 25 years), yet they are useful and lovely in the garden, especially in very early spring (February to March) when they are covered with clouds of yellow flowers.

Tall trees, with shrubs in front of them, frame this garden. The lawn, a beautiful expanse of green, runs the length of the house; close to the house is a fine flower garden accented by a water pool. (Photo by Molly Adams.)

Acer (maple).   Maples are popular shade trees, and there are many kinds for many uses. They are varied in habit and rate of growth, size, and leaf shape—some (such as Japanese maple) are low and squatty; others (such as the Norway maple) are round at the top and quite tall. Smaller varieties are ideal for landscaping in limited space. Some maples have interesting, colorful bark, but it is the autumn color of the foliage—brilliant red or yellow—that makes them popular. Maples grow in any good garden soil and are generally not bothered by pests or diseases.

Albizzia (silk tree).   Often overlooked, albizzia is a small tree with delicate, fernlike foliage and charming summer flowers. Its arching stems and compact growth make it an excellent landscape subject. Albizzia likes sun and a good garden loam that is somewhat sandy. In the North, where it is likely to die down to the ground in winter, remove dead stems early in spring to encourage new growth.

Betula (birch).   Birches are favorite ornamental trees because of their graceful appearance; the most popular ones have handsome white bark, and the bright yellow autumn color is lovely. The trees are somewhat short-lived and are difficult to transplant unless they are balled and burlapped. They must be moved in the spring. Once established, most birches are easy to grow and will thrive in wet or dry soil.

Carya (hickory).   Hickories are robust trees, and once established they grow into giants, not bothered by insects or disease. They are difficult to transplant and should not be moved unless absolutely necessary. In general, hickories are excellent ornamental trees because of their golden autumn foliage. They make superior accents in the garden, if there is space for them. Some are broad in habit; others grow narrow and upright.

Cedrus (cedar).   Cedars are good, big evergreen trees that need lots of space. Their sculptural growth enhances the landscape. They need a somewhat rich soil but are relatively troublefree. Some species are stiff in appearance, but others are more graceful, with pendant branches.

Cercis (redbud).   Redbuds are small, deciduous trees that rarely grow to over 25 feet in height. They have lovely, heart-shaped leaves and clusters of small magenta-pink blossoms in spring. The flowers are long lasting, and foliage turns bright yellow in fall. The redbuds will grow in full sun or light shade and are not particular about soil conditions.

Chamaecyparis (false cypress).   False cypresses are favorite evergreens, with many color forms and varieties. The Japanese species withstand drier atmosphere than do others in the group. Generally dense and pyramidal in shape, these trees are free of insects and disease. They are popular additions to the garden picture and need little care.

A young garden in the Victorian tradition, this plan has a little of everything, formal and informal. Trees, shrubs, and flowers are well placed, and a fine wisteria vine provides a handsome mantle in the background. In time, when the hedges have grown, this will be an attractive garden. (Photo by Matthew Barr.)

Handsome stone containers provide the accent in this Victorian backyard. (Photo by C/D Luckhardt.)

Cornus (dogwood).   Dogwood trees are just about the best small deciduous trees you can find; they grow rapidly, have splendid color when in bloom, and are showy again in autumn with their colorful foliage. There is a dogwood for almost any part of the United States. Some are wide and spreading, with horizontal branches; others are narrow and upright. Many varieties of *C. florida* are offered by nurseries, but not all are good ones, so make choices carefully.

Crataegus (hawthorn).   A widely distributed group of deciduous trees, hawthorns are dense, twiggy, dependable, and loaded with flowers in May. These slow-growing trees are compact and beautiful. Generally, it is their picturesque shape and their bright red fruit in fall that make them so popular. Hawthorns will grow in poor soil, and some keep their fruit all winter.

Fagus (beech).   The deciduous beech is elegant and beautiful all year, especially in fall, when it blazes with golden color. Usually beeches are large, with stout trunks and smooth bark. When you plant beeches, remember that very little can be grown underneath them because they provide much shade.

Fraxinus (ash).   The ash is a rapid-growing deciduous tree that has brilliant yellow to purple foliage in fall. These trees grow large (some to 100 feet) and need lots of space, hardly making them suitable for small properties. Ash trees grow without much attention in any reasonably good soil.

Gingko.   A popular home and street tree, the gingko has fan-shaped leaves that turn bright gold in fall. Known for its open growth habit and height (can grow to 100 feet), it is also very tolerant of adverse conditions, and does well in most situations. A popular species is *G. biloba.*

Juniperus (juniper).   These evergreens are valued for their colorful berries in fall and winter. Both male and female plants must be grown near each other to ensure fruiting. Junipers are tall and dense in habit and prefer a somewhat alkaline soil.

Koelreuteria (golden-rain tree).   A native of China and Japan, this lovely garden tree grows to about 30 feet. The yellow flowers appear in upright clusters in July, and the tree is breathtaking when in bloom. It is extremely tolerant of various soils and does well in most places. The species name is *K. paniculata*; improved varieties are available.

Liquidambar (sweet gum).   This conical-shaped deciduous tree has lustrous, deep green leaves that turn crimson or gold in fall. Sweet gum is known for its lovely branching habit. Bothered by few pests, it generally tolerates most soils and can grow to 70 feet.

Liriodendron (tulip tree).   Popular and lovely, with golden-yellow foliage

This typical small garden of a Victorian house, with its lush ground cover, is accented by a handsome brick patio and container plants. (Photo by C/D Luckhardt.)

in fall, this tree needs well-drained soil and lots of space. It can grow to 80 feet.

Magnolia. A popular group because they have splendid flowers, many magnolias bloom in early spring before the leaves appear. In a wide range of colors—white, pink, red, reddish purple—the flowers are spectacular. Many magnolias are wide-spreading and tall (to 90 feet); others grow only to 30 feet. Some are deciduous, and others are evergreen. There are varieties that have early flowers, and some bloom in summer. Any pruning should be done immediately after flowering.

Malus (crab apple).   Crab apples are good, ornamental, deciduous trees that flower in vivid color in May. Some varieties have single blooms; others have semidouble or double flowers in colors from pure white to purple-red. Many crab apples are fragrant. The fruit of some varieties holds color well into winter, giving the trees a two-season value. Most crab apples are small, to about 30 feet, although a few reach to 50 feet. Several have pendant branches, but actually shapes run the gamut from columnar to round-headed. Crab apples need sun and, when young, require some additional feeding. A regular schedule of spraying is necessary because these trees have the same problems as does the common apple—fire blight, scale, and borers.

Picea (spruce).   Young spruce trees make a pretty picture in the landscape, but mature ones generally lose their lower branches and become unsightly. Because most spruces grow to about 100 feet, they are not for the small garden; still, there are some good evergreens in the group.

Pinus (pine).   Some pines are better than others for ornamental use. The evergreen needles vary in length on each tree but are usually from 2 to 12 inches long. Some pines are dwarf in stature and very picturesque, others are open and shrubby in habit, and still others are rounded. Many appear graceful in the landscape, although a few are quite stiff and hardly desirable. Make your selection carefully.

Quercus (oak).   Oaks are sturdy, long-lived trees valued for their autumn color; the majority reach a large size. Only the North American species have autumn color. The oaks are fine shade trees for large properties, but they can have their problems—borers, oak gall, various leaf diseases—and so must be sprayed routinely. The wood is strong and does not split easily.

Salix (willow).   The deciduous willows like water and moist conditions. Although the weeping willow is certainly graceful and lovely, remember that in many regions willows are troubled with insects and disease and have weak wood that cracks easily.

Taxus (yew).   Dark green evergreen trees that thrive in many different kinds of soil, yews are tough to kill. Some yews make excellent hedges and screens, and they bear bright red fruit in fall. Most yews are slow-growing.

Thuja (arborvitae).   Generally having flat, scalelike leaves, the evergreen arborvitaes are quite shrubby and somewhat pyramidal in shape. They don't tolerate dry conditions, preferring moisture at the roots and in the air. A few are unsatisfactory because their leaves turn brown in winter. For the most part, this group is slow-growing.

Tilia (linden).   Lindens are excellent deciduous trees—possibly the best ones for shade, although they excel in other areas too. They have handsome heart-shaped leaves and lovely, sweet-scented pendulous flowers in early summer. As a group, the lindens have much to offer and require very little attention.

Tsuga (hemlock).   These narrow-leaved evergreens are beautiful, but they need a great deal of water. All withstand shade but will grow better with some sun. The Japanese hemlock is possibly the best of the group. All hemlocks bear small cones, but not every year. Many varieties are offered.

SHRUBS

Few shrubs were used in Victorian times, in comparison with our use of them today. Most had a difficult time in the moist English climate; this fact, together with their limited availability, probably accounts for their sparse use.

Rhododendrons were perhaps the most popular shrub, followed by kalmia, ilex, and mahonia, all referred to often in Victorian gardening books. It was not until the early 1900s that broader use was made of shrubs, including berberis, cotoneaster, and philadelphus.

Most people race out and plant flowers and bulbs or lawns and forget shrubs. Yet these plants can create pleasing gardens. At first they may seem small and scrawny, but soon shrubs grow into lovely plants that can be pruned and trained to your specifications. Like vines, shrubs cover a multitude of sins in the garden, and most shrubs have a robust nature, growing even in untoward conditions. Plant them deep, soak the soil thoroughly, and always use good topsoil with supplemental feeding.

There are low-, medium-, and tall-growing shrubs. It is tempting to plant any group of shrubs without respect to their height, but this can be disastrous in a few years. Select your shrubs according to height, and use them as functional pieces of architecture rather than just as plants. As with trees, place shrubs in groups, with the taller ones in the background and shorter ones up front to create visual interest. Follow the premise of Chapter 2: never block views, and use shrubs to create vistas. If there is a particularly nice view, put a group of shrubs to one side, with another group on the other side, but not equally spaced. This creates a viewing alley and makes a handsome picture, directing the eye to the scene beyond. If the view beyond is not pleasing, go against the rules and use your shrubs to block the eyesore. Or, if your garden is too public, plant shrubs for privacy.

Do not mix and match shrubs. Use three or five of one kind in one area to make a statement, otherwise you will have a spotty and unkempt effect. A mass of color is far more handsome than a blob of color here and there,

An entrance to a Victorian house today: even this small bed of flowers is a perfect foil for the iron railings and stone walls. (Photo by C/D Luckhardt.)

and massing shrubs saves pruning. Single shrubs have to be pruned almost constantly to keep them in a handsome shape, but groups of shrubs cover each other.

There are flowering shrubs, evergreen shrubs, shrubs for autumn color, shrubs for the winter, shrubs for hedges and topiaries, and shrubs for soil retention and sound barriers. There are literally hundreds of shrubs you can plant. The following list of popular shrub families and their members is as simple as possible but includes all important aspects of shrubs: height, width, good characteristics, and so on.

LIST OF SHRUBS

BERBERIS (barberry).   Berberis is a group of dense and thorny deciduous and evergreen shrubs, with small, bright flowers. These plants are effective as barriers, but they can also be used as landscape specimens because many species have a lovely branching habit. Small bright red or purple-black berries appear in autumn. Most barberries lose their fruit quickly after it ripens, but the Japanese barberry holds its color through winter. These shrubs grow in almost any kind of soil, in sun or light shade, and so are very useful.

B. *buxifolia* (Magellan barberry) is hardy to −10°F, and grows upright to 6 feet, with small, leathery leaves. It has orange-yellow flowers and dark purple berries, and is evergreen.

B. *gagnepainii* (black barberry) is hardy to −10°F, grows to 8 feet, and has thorny twigs and rangy growth. Has narrow leaves and blue-black berries and is evergreen.

B. *koreana* (Korean barberry) is hardy to −10°F and grows to 6 feet. It has deep red autumn color in fall and winter, and yellow flowers in May. This shrub is deciduous.

B. *mentorensis* (mentor barberry) is a hybrid, hardy to −10°F; grows to 5 feet; evergreen in some regions, deciduous in others. It has dark red berries and yellow flowers.

B. *thunbergii* "Erecta" (Japanese barberry) is hardy to −5°F. Graceful in growth, with arching stems, it has deep green foliage and fiery red berries in fall. This shrub is deciduous; there are many varieties.

B. *verruculosa* (warty barberry) is hardy to −10°F, has a neat habit and grows to about 4 feet. This evergreen has glossy, dark green leaves and golden yellow flowers.

COTONEASTER.   Cotoneaster shrubs grow under untoward conditions (but do not tolerate full shade) and still produce good growth. The bright red berries are handsome, and the white or pink flowers are a charming asset to the garden. Many species have interesting growth habits, making them good landscape subjects. Some cotoneasters are deciduous; others are semideciduous; and still others are evergreen. Many are native to the cool regions of China. In dry, hot weather, the plants are susceptible to red spider or lace bug attacks, which must be kept under control or the shrubs may die.

C. apiculata (cranberry cotoneaster) is hardy to −20°F and grows to 4 feet. It has bright green leaves, pink-white flowers, and red fruit, and is deciduous.

C. conspicua (wintergreen cotoneaster) is hardy to −5°F and grows to 6 feet. It has oval, dark green leaves, white flowers, arching branches, bright red fruit, and is evergreen.

C. dammeri (barberry cotoneaster) is hardy to −10°F. It has a prostrate trailing habit and oval, bright green leaves, white flowers, and red fruit. This beautiful, cascading plant is evergreen.

C. divaricata (spreading cotoneaster) is hardy to −10°F and grows to 6 feet. It has stiff branches, dark green leaves and pink flowers followed by red fruit. It makes a good hedge or screen and is deciduous.

C. horizontalis (rock spray cotoneaster) is hardy to −10°F and is low, growing to 3 feet, but spreading, with stiff branches. Its small and glossy bright green leaves, white flowers, and red fruit make it a good bank cover or espalier subject. This cotoneaster is deciduous.

C. microphylla (small-leaf cotoneaster) is hardy to −10°F; somewhat trailing, it grows to 3 feet tall. Its small green leaves and white flowers are followed by large red fruit. Evergreen, it makes good ground cover (see next chapter).

C. pannosa (silverleaf cotoneaster) is hardy to −5°F; an erect shrub that grows to 10 feet. Its oval gray-green leaves, white flowers, and red fruit make it a good screen plant. This variety is evergreen; semievergreen in the coldest weather zones.

C. rotundifolia (redbox cotoneaster) is hardy to −5°F; grows erect to 10 feet. It has dark green, glossy leaves, white flowers, and large red fruit. Redbox cotoneaster is a good screening plant, and is evergreen or semi-deciduous.

EUONYMUS (euonymus). Although the flowers of this group are small and insignificant, their autumn foliage color is spectacular. Plants grow vigorously in any good garden soil, but they are susceptible to scale and must be sprayed regularly. Some euonymous in this group are vines, whereas others are shrubs. Most are excellent landscape subjects.

This small garden is handsome in itself, but with the addition of the Greek column, the scene takes on elegance and beauty. (Photo by Scharmer.)

E. alata (winged euonymus) is hardy to −35°F, and has a horizontal and branching habit. It grows to 10 feet, with dark green leaves that turn red in fall (deciduous). The "Compacta" is an excellent dwarf plant, growing to 4 feet.

E. bungeanus semipersistens (midwinter euonymus) is hardy to −20°F and grows vigorously, to 15 feet. It has light green leaves and yellow to whitish-pink flowers. This euonymus is a good hedge plant and is deciduous.

E. fortunei is hardy to −10°F. It grows as a vine or shrub to 15 feet with dark green leaves (evergreen). The "Berryhill" grows upright, as does the "Sarcoxie" — to 4 feet.

E. japonica is hardy to 10°F; grows upright to 10 feet. It has lustrous green leaves, pinkish orange fruit, and is evergreen. The "Albo-Marginata" has green leaves edged white, and the "Grandifolia" has large, dark green leaves.

E. latifolius (broadleaf euonymus) is hardy to −10°F; its leaves reddish underneath, and it bears red to orange fruit. This deciduous shrub grows to 20 feet.

ILEX (holly). The hollies can be either evergreen or deciduous and are very popular because they are amenable plants. European and American hollies have hundreds of varieties. The bright red or black berries are highly desirable for landscape color. With a few exceptions, hollies have separate sexes, so both must be present in the area to ensure the fertilization of flowers. (Chinese holly can produce fruit without the pollen of other hollies.) Most plants grow easily in a good garden soil, but they do need good drainage; they are relatively free of pests and diseases.

I. aquifolium (English holly) is hardy to −5°F and grows to 15 feet. It is variable in leaf, shape, and color, and there are many varieties (all evergreen).

I. cornuta (Chinese holly) is hardy to 5°F; grows dense or open to 10 feet. It has glossy, leathery leaves, bright red berries, and is evergreen. The "Burfordii" has spineless leaves, the "Dazzler" is compact and has many berries, the "Giant Beauty" is upright and large, and the "Jungle Gardens" bears yellow fruit.

I. crenata (Japanese holly) is hardy to −5 F. It grows dense and erect, sometimes to 20 feet. This holly has finely toothed evergreen leaves and black berries. The "Compacta" is densely branched, the "Green Island" is low and spreading, and the "Microphylla" has tiny leaves.

I. glabra (inkberry) is hardy to −35°F, grows to 9 feet, has black berries, and is evergreen.

I. verticillata (winterberry) is hardy to −35°F. It grows to 10 feet, bears bright red berries, and is deciduous.

LIGUSTRUM (privet). Privets are popular hedge plants. The leaves may be evergreen (in the South) or deciduous. Vigorous and fast-growing, with small white flowers followed by blue or black berries, they also make good specimen plants against a fence or a wall. Most of the privets are remarkably free of problems, and they grow in almost any kind of soil under all kinds of conditions. There are many privets, one hardly distinguishable from the other until they are mature, so ask your nurseryman about them before making purchases.

L. amurense (Amur privet) is hardy to −35°F and deciduous in the North, evergreen in the South. It grows to 15 feet, with small spikes of white flowers and small black berries. It is similar to California privet, but hardier.

L. japonicum (Japanese privet) is hardy to 5°F. It grows densely, to 12 feet, with clusters of small white flowers, and is evergreen. The "Lusterleaf" (texanum) has very large leaves.

L. lucidum (glossy privet) is hardy to 5°F. This round-headed shrub can reach 30 feet. It has small white flowers, black berries, and is evergreen.

L. ovalifolium (California privet) is hardy to −10°F. It has creamy white flowers and bears black berries (except in the North). This semideciduous shrub grows to 15 feet. The "Aureum" (golden privet) has leaves with yellow edges.

L. vulgare (common privet) is hardy to −20°F and grows to 15 feet. It has clusters of white flowers, black berries, and is deciduous. The "Pyramidale" is an excellent hedge plant.

VINES

Vines were a "natural" for the Victorians; their flowing lines and curving dimensions contributed grace and beauty. Their foliage was handsome and their flowers dramatic, and as a result vines as decorative items became very popular in Victorian garden planning. Trained on trellises and arbors, they enriched a setting with color and provided the ornate quality so popular in that era.

As garden features, vines add quality and character to a garden—they are the missing vertical element to complement trees, and they are almost as versatile as shrubs. Vines will go up or down, cover windows and unsightly corners, clothe fences in color, wrap around walls, and so on. We should use more vines in our gardens today to create the decorative appeal we expect from the outdoors.

Some climbing vines—such as clematis and morning glory—can, with proper care, become screens of living color, and vines such as stephanotis, wisteria, and sweet pea (a favorite with the Victorians) have a dainty love-

Statuary and urns such as those popular in the early 1900s lend a Victorian flair to the entrance of this house. (Photo by Robert Toubol.)

liness that is often necessary to soften harsh garden walls and house lines. And many vines—among them bittersweet—have colorful winter berries that are lovely against the gray skies of winter.

Some vines climb by means of twining stems that need support; others have tendrils or discs for climbing. Some have leaflike appendages that act as tendrils, grasping objects for support. Other plants, such as jasmine, have long, slender arching stems and need support; and some, such as ivy geranium and trailing lantana, grow prostrate. Vines may be open and delicate, or heavy with masses of foliage. Several kinds grow rapidly, in a few months—others take years to fill a space.

LIST OF VINES

Aristolochia durior (Dutchman's pipe) can grow to 30 feet with little trouble and is perfect for covering arbors and trellises. The big, dark green, heart-shaped leaves are attractive, but the unique flowers are more bizarre than beautiful. It needs a good soil to prosper but will grow in either sun or shade. It is hardy to -20 to $-10°F$.

Bignonia (flame vine), also called *Clystoma* in the trade, is a lovely vine with fine red or orange funnel-shaped flowers. Slow to start, bignonia eventually covers fast and provides a lush display. It is invasive and will crawl over anything; yet in the right situation it is a superlative plant. It is hardy to -20 to $-10°F$.

Celastrus scandens (false bittersweet) has orange-yellow flowers and

51

handsome foliage—a good vine selection. The plant grows in almost any garden soil in sun or shade. It is hardy to −50 to −35°F.

Clematis virginia (clematis) has graceful leaves and handsome flowers. It likes a good soil and a partially sunny place where it can grow to 20 feet or more. Many new clematis varieties are available now. It is hardy to −20 to −10°F.

Gelsemium sempervirens (Carolina yellow jasmine) is a fine, dark green vine that has lovely yellow flowers. It grows vigorously and makes a fine display. This jasmine likes partial sun and average soils and is hardy to −5 to 5°F.

Lonicera (honeysuckle) is a vigorous grower and needs a strong support. Several species are available—perhaps *L. sempervirens*, with handsome green leaves and tubular scarlet or orange flowers, is best. It grows readily in partial shade and is hardy to −35 to −20°F.

Parthenocissus quinquefolia (Virginia creeper) has compound leaves that turn red in fall, making this a worthwhile addition to the garden picture. It is a fine subject for covering walls or buildings. Virginia creeper grows in either sun or shade and in almost any kind of soil. It is hardy to −35 to −20°F.

Passiflora incarnata (passion flower) has many varieties, all handsome vines with exquisite flowers. They need sun and a humus-rich soil and are hardy to −5 to 5°F.

Vitis (grape) grow quickly with minimal care. There are grapes for almost all climate zones, and more people should grow them for their handsome decorative effect. Check to see what kinds are available from local growers.

FLOWERS

The Victorians' use of flowers was a crowning achievement perpetuated in the English gardens of today. At the beginning of this vogue, it was suggested that potted plants be plunged in beds for their time of color and then replaced with others, a technique called *bedding out*. This was easily accomplished in Victorian England: tender plants could be wintered in greenhouses and plants could be forced and then planted outside after the hardy spring flowers faded. When summer bloom was over, those flowers that bloomed in autumn were displayed.

A foreground of flowers, formerly used merely to frame what lay beyond, became for the Victorians a focal point of the garden. Beds of flowers in the shape of the great arabesques of French parterres or stars, crescents, and baskets dotted lawns in English gardens. Yet for all this beauty, the jubilant but haphazard use of color sometimes created jarring effect. Only after a

Phlox

Zinnia

Bachelor's Button

ANNUALS

time did a clearer understanding of color reduce flower beds to their proper place in the garden.

Annuals and perennials are the prime flowers for Victorian gardens, with biennials and bulbs as supplements. Annuals and perennials (also called *bedding plants*) may be used, as they were in Victorian times, in (1) narrow beds bordering a straight walk, (2) a variety of beds of generally symmetrical patterns, and (3) as an embellishment to a lawn or group of shrubs.

To border a walk, plant flowers in beds 4 feet wide. The beds act as a finishing, framing touch and are quite attractive unless the flowers become straggly and overgrow the walk. Because flowers planted in straight rows can visually dissect the garden, giving it a separate look that is not desirable, make flower beds that border paths and walks curved or arced. They will then provide some grace and continuity.

Flower beds in symmetrical patterns — *drifts*, as I prefer to call them — near lawns are very pleasing, because the flowers grow into a mass of color and create dramatic visual attractions. The beds should be large enough to have a concentration of plants — not just 4 or 5, but 50 or 100. The beds should never appear to cut up or dissect the lawn; they should create their own entity. Also, these drifts should be repeated in the overall balance and proportion. One flower bed nestled near a lawn can be incongruous, but three curved and graceful beds placed strategically unify the garden plan. Plant the drifts so there is enough open lawn behind them.

Keeping a great number of flower beds filled with summer- and fall-blooming plants is expensive and involves a fair amount of maintenance, including trimming. The best solution seems to be a good stand of perennials interspersed with annuals. Use concentrated masses of one particular flower next to other masses, and so on. Never stick in just a few plants here and there or the effect will be spotty and unappealing. A grand display can be had, but it does take work, so be prepared.

As with other plants, choose your flowers carefully. Place tall ones in the back, medium growers in the middle, and low-growing species at the front, for a gradation of height. Plant flowers as you might build a terrace — in tiers, for dimension and eye interest. As you plant for height, also allow for flower form: round, pyramidal, and so on. Use similarly shaped flowers together; round ones next to star-shaped ones, for example, just do not look good.

In addition, select flower colors so there is no jarring effect to the eye. Use gradations of color just as you use gradations of height. That is, if you have orange blooms, use orange-red flowers next to them, and then red flowers. If you move from, for example, yellow to red flowers, the change is too abrupt.

Candytuft

Marigold

Cineraria

ANNUALS

You can also use annuals and perennials as links to lawns, shrubs, and trees, to create a marriage with other plants.

If you use flowers in any of the ways just described but for some reason they do not create quite the effect you want, embellish the scene a bit with statuary and urns. These were very popular in Victorian times, and they sometimes add just the right note to the flower areas. Sometimes there is so much drama in a flower area that you need *more* drama. If you make it overwhelming, the entire play then becomes acceptable. This may sound rather facetious, but it works.

LIST OF ANNUALS

Ageratum (floss flower). *Ageratum houstonianum* (Aj-er-RAY-tum hew-STONE-ee-aynum). This flower has blue, white, or pink varieties. It is available from 4 to 22 inches tall and has many uses, blooming from early summer until fall. Ageratum forms compact mounds of foliage. It needs well-drained soil and somewhat heavy watering.

Alyssum. *Lobularia maritima* (Lo-byu-LAR-ee-a mar-RIT-im-uh). Available in several colors, this low-growing annual is generally used as an edging plant. It has a multitude of uses in the garden when combined with other plants or used as a filler around perennials. Alyssum will grow in hot, dry situations if necessary.

Aster, China Aster. *Callistephus chinensis* (Kal-LISS-tef-us chin-NEN-siss). These 1- to 3-foot plants have wiry stems and beautiful white to deep red flowers. Some are early blooming, others bloom in midseason, and still others provide late color. They are one of the best flowers for cutting.

Bachelor's Button, Cornflower. *Centaurea cyanus* (Sen-taw-REE-uh sye-AY-nus). Growing to a height of 2½ feet, these fine plants bear pink, white, wine, or blue flowers. Their gray-green foliage makes a dramatic display, and although they require pinching and pruning they bloom profusely.

Calendula, Pot Marigold. *Calendula officinalis* (Kal-END-yew-luh off-iss-in-NAY-liss). These well-known, bright, rounded flowers come in a variety of colors: orange, cream, or gold. Pot marigolds grow 12 to 24 inches tall and bloom all summer. They grow with almost no care and are a workhorse of the garden.

Candytuft. *Iberis umbellata* (Eye-BER-iss um-bel-LAY-tuh). Masses of flowers make candytuft a good choice for the beginning gardener. The plants mound to 12 or 15 inches, and in late spring and early summer bloom profusely. Flower color may be pink, salmon, or white. Candytuft is good for cutting or garden display.

Impatiens

Dianthus

Hollyhock

ANNUALS

Cineraria. *Senecio cruentus* (Sen-NEE-see-oh krew-EN-tus). This annual will bloom in shade. The daisylike flowers come in light or dark shades of blue or purple and magenta. The plants grow from 12 to 15 inches and have handsome foliage. Keep them shady and moist, in well-drained soil.

Coleus. *Coleus blumei* (KOH-lee-us BLUE-mee-eye). Coleus is a foliage plant that comes in a multitude of colors. The tapestry-colored, toothed leaves are an asset in any garden, and plants can reach to 3 feet or more. Pinch growing tips to make them compact. Coleus is a good background plant.

Hollyhock. *Althaea rosea* (Al-thee-uh ROH-zee-uh). Neglected in recent years, hollyhocks are making a reappearance in gardens, and I recommend them because they are so colorful and can survive in practically any situation. They grow to 6 feet, with large flowers in a spectrum of color: pink, rose, yellow, red, and white. (Hollyhocks are generally classed as biennials, but it is best to start them fresh every year.)

Impatiens. *Impatiens balsamina* (Im-PAT-ee-enz bal-SAY-meen-uh). These plants have many virtues in the garden; they come in many different colors and heights and bloom profusely. They like some sun but also succeed in shade.

Marigold. *Tagetes erecta* (Taj-JEET-eez ee-RECT-ah). These all-time favorites grow quickly, come in all sizes from 6 to 40 inches, and bloom constantly from summer to fall. The blossoms come in many shades of yellow, orange, dark red, and maroon and can be used by themselves for lovely accents or with other plantings. There are many types: French dwarf to 18 inches in a five array of color, African dwarf to 16 inches, and some new varieties. Most types need an evenly moist soil in a sunny place.

Nasturtium. *Tropaeoleum majus* (Trop-PEE-o-le-um MA-jus). The under-rated nasturtiums can bring an immense wealth of color to the garden, and easier plants to grow cannot be found. Nasturtiums bloom from early summer until frost and now come in single, semidouble, or double flowers in shades of yellow, orange, crimson, pink, maroon, and multicolored varieties. Dwarf plants can be used for borders, taller varieties for spot color. Most nasturtiums will crowd out weeds and grow rapidly with little care.

Phlox. *Phlox drummondii* (FLOX drum-MON-dee-eye). These annuals, which grow to 16 inches, have lovely clusters of 1-inch flowers. The choice of color includes rose, crimson, salmon, white, scarlet, and violet, often with contrasting eyes. They bloom abundantly and are seldom bothered by insects. Phlox grows in sun with plenty of water.

Pink, Sweet William. *Dianthus* (Dye-ANTH-us). There are so many varieties of pinks that you may be confused, but do try them. They have

Aster

Chrysanthemum

Baby's Breath

PERENNIALS

clusters of pink or white flowers. Pinks are easy to grow and are available in many heights.

Snapdragon. *Antirrhinum majus* (An-ti-RY-num MA-jus). Snapdragons are tall, stately, lovely annuals with beguiling flowers; there are many colors to choose from (except blue). Snapdragons come in many heights and make superb vertical accents in the garden. They will tolerate some shade but prefer sun. To increase bloom yield, cut flowers frequently and remove faded blossoms. There are many varieties in many sizes.

Zinnia. *Zinnia elegans* (ZINN-ee-uh ELL-eg-anz). This popular annual has many sizes, forms, heights, and colors. Zinnias have infinite uses in the garden and are fast growers that need little care, but plenty of moisture. Flower colors include orange, yellow, pink, red, lavender, and some bicolors.

LIST OF PERENNIALS

Aster, New England Aster. *Aster frikartii* (AST-er fra-CART-ee), *Aster novae-angliae* (AST-er NO-vay-ON-glay). Their dramatic blue and purple flowers make these two perennials outstanding. The daisylike flowers, which are produced in abundance, are bright and showy. The plants are available in several heights and make fine displays in large drifts. Asters like lots of sun and water.

Baby's Breath. *Gypsophila paniculata* (Jip-SOFF-il-uh pa-NICK-you-lah-tah). These dainty, lacy plants grow rapidy to 2 feet and bear small, rounded white flowers in masses. (There are also pink-and-white varieties.) The blooms last over a month, and the plants make excellent garden fillers.

Basket of Gold. *Alyssum saxatile* (A-LISS-um SACKS-uh-teal). Splashes of golden flowers make this a pretty garden plant. Foliage is gray and provides an interesting contrast in the garden. (Don't confuse this plant with the annual sweet alyssum, which is called *Lobularia*.)

Bellflower. *Campanula persicifolia* (Kam-PAN-yew-luh per-SICK-ee-fol-ee-ah). These should be grown more often because they offer so much color. With their white or blue flowers in June ahd July, they form mounds of color and grow to 10 inches. Give the plants full sun or light shade, and be sure they are in well-drained soil.

Blanketflower. *Gaillardia aristata* (Gay-LARD-ee-ah air-ih-sta-TUH). Gaillardias produce showy flowers over a long period of time. The blooms are daisylike and generally bright yellow, although bronzy scarlet types have also been introduced. Undemanding, they do best in a slightly sandy soil with adequate sun.

Bugloss. *Anchusa azurea* (An-KEW-suh AYX-your-ee-ah). Clusters of bright blue blossoms make bugloss an outstanding addition in the garden.

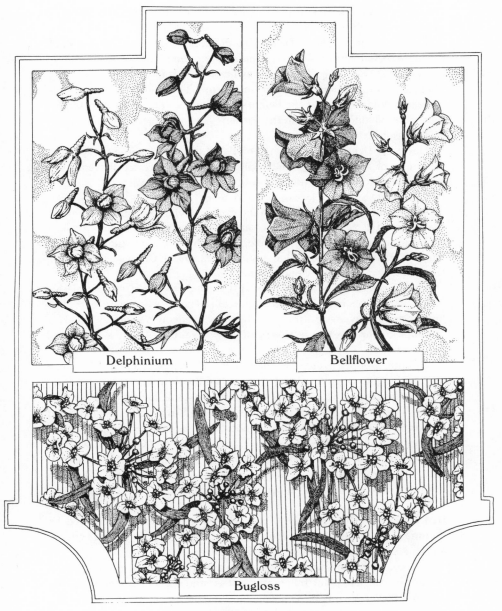

Delphinium

Bellflower

Bugloss

PERENNIALS

The plants can grow to 6 feet. Some excellent new varieties are now available.

Chrysanthemum; Shasta Daisy. *Chrysanthemum maximum* (Kriss-ANTH-e-mum MAX-uh-mum); *Chrysanthemum morifolium* (Kriss-ANTH-e-mum more-uh-FOAL-ee-um). These are available in a multitude of colors and shapes: spoon, cushion, pompom, and button. The colors vary from white to yellow, gold, or orange; the heights are variable. There are chrysanthemums for all kinds of uses in the garden. They will tolerate dry soils and still flourish.

Day Lily. *Hemerocallis* (Hem-er-oh-KALLis). These large plants have fountains of grassy foliage and yellow, cream, or bronze flowers. The plants start blooming in May and continue on and off until frost. Most are tall and rangy and need lots of sun and space.

Delphinium; Larkspur. *Delphinium elatum* (Del-FIN-ee-um ee-LA-tum). Handsome, tall plants with spires of large flowers, delphiniums are excellent for background plantings. Their colors range from white to pink to superb blues. Rich, well-drained soil and sun are essential. Chinese delphinium (*D. grandiflorum*) is also handsome.

False Spirea. *Astilbe japonica* (As-TIL-be Jap-ON-ik-ah). A perennial for shady places, this plant has white, pink, or red flowers on wiry stems. The bronze-green leaves are attractive; the bloom season is summer. Ideal for mixing with shrubby plants, this plant grows to about 24 inches. Moist soil is essential.

Oriental Poppy. *Papaver orientale* (Pap-AY-ver or-ee-en-TUL). These are coming into popularity again, and it is difficult to find more dramatic flowers than their bold orange blooms. Once established, they bloom profusely. The plants are 2 to 4 feet high, with 6- to 8-inch flowers. They need well-drained soil and some sun, but not direct, intense sun.

Summer Phlox, Moss Pink. *Phlox subulata* (FLOX SUB-you-la-tuh). These 3- to 5-foot plants bear a wealth of large pink flowers. Phlox are compatible with most garden flowers and make splendid accents. They do, however, need deep, fertile soil and sun to prosper.

BULBS. For the gardener who wants early spring color followed by summer beauty, bulb flowers are excellent. Bulbs are planted and covered and that's that—usually there is no battle with the bugs.

Crocus, narcissus, and snowdrops, planted in early fall, are first up in spring. In late fall, plant tulips and scillas, and then in spring plant the summer-flowering bulbs. You can have bulbs blooming in the garden almost all year. They impart a nostalgic feeling to the scene—popular decades ago and still highly favored by gardeners.

Blanket Flower

Astilbe

Day Lily

Oriental Poppy

Summer Phlox

PERENNIALS

Many of the most beautiful bulbs are winter-hardy and are left in the ground all year, year after year—they need cold weather to grow. Others must be planted and lifted each year. The life cycle of a bulb includes blooming, foliage growth when food is stored in the bulb, and resting time.

All bulbs need a moisture-retentive but rapid draining soil with high organic matter. They do not grow well in sandy soil, and few thrive in clay. Dig holes for bulbs with caution; they should be concave, rather than pointed holes that leave an air pocket below the bulb. There is some confusion among amateur gardeners about which end of the bulb goes into the ground and how deep to plant it. A 3-inch depth means that the bulb has its top, not its bottom, 3 inches below ground level. Plant the growing side up; this is the pointed end or the end showing growth. Firm the soil over the bulb; do not leave it loose.

Buy top-quality bulbs from reputable dealers and avoid bargains. You are buying an unseen product and must trust the dealer to give you healthy, robust bulbs that will bloom for years rather than tired bulbs that may come up blind (without flowers).

Bulbs can live off their own storehouse of food for some time, but they should not be neglected when they are actively growing. Water them regularly from the time they start growing until after the flowers have faded. Then taper off watering gradually rather than abruptly. Dormant bulbs do not need any more water than natural conditions provide for them. Spring bulbs can be fertilized twice a season, and summer bulbs are fertilized as soon as they show growth and then again in the few weeks before they bloom. Use a balanced feeding mixture with a low nitrogen content.

Spring bulbs bear color in late winter or early spring; they are left in the ground all year and are called *hardy bulbs*. However, bulbs hardy in one climate may not be so in another region. Spring bulbs are usually put into the ground from September until the ground freezes.

With spring bulbs, remember that after the flowers fade, the foliage must ripen naturally for several weeks. Do not cut off the leaves. Common spring bulbs for your Victorian garden are listed on pages 157–58.

In most of the United States, summer-flowering bulbs (see list on pages 158–59) must be dug up in fall and stored over winter in a dry, cool place. They can be left in the ground only if temperatures do not go below freezing. Most of these bulbs are planted in the ground after the danger of frost is over. When the foliage dies down in the fall, dig up summer bulbs and let them dry off in an airy place.

5.

LAWNS AND GROUND COVERS

To the Victorians, a good lawn was a necessity. The idea of a parklike garden still prevailed; only when you had a lawn could you have a garden. It is true that there is nothing quite like a carpet of green to enrich a garden setting. Even a small lawn creates the ambience we expect in a garden.

LAWN CONSIDERATIONS

How much work and time are involved in lawns? Initially, a lot; however, once established—this may take anywhere from 3 to 12 months—a good lawn takes care of itself.

Is your lawn just for show, or do you want to be able to stroll and play on it? Some grasses are better for walking than others, and there are grasses for all situations and all regions. Bent grass has a finely textured appearance and is excellent for golf greens but impossible to maintain for the average home.

Use the type of grass that does best in your climate. Consider, too, whether your site is sunny or shady. Some grasses can grow in semi-shade, but most need sun. If the area is completely shaded, grow a ground cover instead of a lawn. Many ground covers succeed in shade where grass will not.

When you select lawn seed, read the package label, because the stated percentage of germination is quite important. It should not be lower than 80 percent; 90 percent is better. Buy the best seed you can afford; inferior seed only leads to disappointment.

A good lawn depends on proper site preparation: leveling any mounds or depressions and providing good drainage.

Finally, know when to plant. Start your lawn in the spring or early fall. In the spring, the good weather is on the way, and in the fall there are fewer temperature fluctuations, so lawns can be established more easily.

PREPARING THE SITE.   Decide where the lawn will be and scout the area on foot. Define the perimeter by connecting corner stakes with string. Now dig. And dig you must—at least 8 to 12 inches—to loosen compacted soil that will not take water. You can dig with a spade or have the ground rototilled.

After you have prepared the site and dug the soil, recondition the subsoil by working organic matter (humus or compost) into it. You can buy humus in sacks at nurseries, or you can prepare your own compost from decayed organic matter like leaves and grass. Next, level the site by raking it. The soil bed should be loose but with some tilth (porosity), so do not rake too much. Now add at least 4 inches of topsoil.

If you are establishing a lawn where trees are already growing, provide "wells" for the trees, to keep the soil from piling up over the root area. Or, easier still, slope the surface soil up to the trees (grade away from the trees). Remember that grass may not grow under surface-rooting shade trees.

METHODS OF PLANTING

SOWING THE SEED.   You can sow lawn seed by hand or with a spreader. Before you sow seed, water the soil slightly, and then let it dry out. Try to sow seed evenly so that the lawn will have uniform growth. Too much seed in one place will produce thick growth, and too little seed will result in sparse growth. If you sow by hand, mix a little soil or sand with the seed to help spread the seed evenly. Always sow on a calm day, because wind can scatter seed unevenly.

Once the seed is spread, rake it lightly. Then roll the seed with a roller or simply leave it. (Rolling may compact the seed into the soil, which is undesirable.)

In the "good old days" a lawn like this could often be seen. Today, however, its maintenance would be too monumental a task.

Now water the seed with a light misting—a strong spray of water will wash away the seed. Mist often and slowly. The soil must be kept evenly moist for the seed to germinate. If the soil is too dry, the seed will die; if the soil is too moist, the seed will succumb to disease.

Birds will eat the grass seed so put a mulch over the area after you sow seed. Use a light covering of grass clippings or peat moss. Peat moss not only protects the seed from birds, it decays naturally, adding nutrients to the soil.

The lawn, combined with the ferns in the foreground, creates an incredibly lush, green feeling. (Photo by Marjorie Dietz.)

In one to three weeks, the seed will germinate and the grass will start growing. As the grass gets higher, you can water less, but do not let the lawn get bone dry. Once the lawn becomes established, feed it twice a month.

INSTANT LAWNS.   You can also establish a lawn by sodding, stripping, or plugging. In these instances you are buying an already established lawn. This saves time and labor, of course, but instant lawns are expensive — exorbitantly so if you have a large area to cover. For reasonably sized areas and spot gardens, however, the instant lawns may be ideal. But remember that you must still prepare a good soil bed.

Sod is mature grass that is ready to be put on the site. It comes in 12- by 12-inch sheets, generally about 1 inch thick. Lay the pieces of sod flush with each other on the prepared bed. Then tamp down or roll the sod evenly and water it thoroughly. For the first few weeks, water the sod carefully: a gentle sprinkling every other day if the weather is dry and warm. Once the sod has taken hold, routine watering is fine.

The stripping process is similar to sodding except that the pieces of sod, 4 to 6 inches wide, are spaced 3 to 6 inches apart. The idea is for the grass strips to spread and create an even lawn. The problem with stripping is that the exposed soil between the strips usually becomes a meeting ground for all the weeds in the neighborhood, making weeding necessary.

In plugging, grass "patches" of 2 to 4 square inches are set into predug holes about 12 to 16 inches apart. Again, constant weeding is necessary because of the exposed soil between plugs. As with a sown lawn, the plugged area must be constantly and evenly moistened, to allow the grass to spread. In six to nine months, the plugs create a green carpet.

CARING FOR YOUR LAWN

WATERING.   Once the lawn is established, water it thoroughly. Note, however, that a gentle sprinkling of water is often better than thorough soakings every week or ten days. The idea is to keep the lawn moist but never soggy. But thorough sprinkling requires time — at least four hours for the water to penetrate 20 inches. Thus you cannot water the lawn with a hose; use a manual or automatic sprinkler.

FEEDING.   In addition to moisture, grass needs plenty of nitrogen (about 20 percent) to prosper. Bermuda grass and bent grass need more feeding than do other grasses. Select a packaged lawn food at your nursery. Use a mechanical spreader to spread the food evenly; otherwise there may be dark green streaks where the lawn has been fertilized and yellow areas where it has not. Feed lawns in the spring and summer — in early summer in the North, and throughout the summer in the South. A lawn exhausts food quickly, so twice-a-month feedings are not excessive for established lawns.

MOWING.   Once the lawn is growing, start mowing it. Do not let the grass get too tall, because cutting high grass shocks it and hinders its growth. A good power or hand mower is essential, one with sharp blades and in tiptop condition. Dull blades can injure grass.

Some gardeners leave short lawn clippings on the grass, because they say it improves the soil, but others believe that clippings left on the turf encourage disease. Cut the grass evenly, but never cut away too much of the vital green leaves; low-cut grass tends to look shaggy. Here are six guidelines for cutting lengths:

1. Cut Kentucky bluegrass 1½ to 2 inches.
2. Cut Merion Kentucky blue 1 to 1¼ inches.
3. Cut bent grass ½ to ¾ of an inch.
4. Do not let grass grow more than 1 inch before cutting it again.
5. Start mowing grass in the spring and continue to the fall or until growth stops.
6. Do not let the lawn go into winter with a thick mat, or disease may start.

COMBATING WEEDS.   Weeds are perennial (lasting two years) or annual, and broadleaf or grassy. Broadleaf weeds include chickweed, carpetweed, dandelion, dock, cress, purslane, pennywort, and plantain. These plants can be pulled out of the soil without too much struggle. Control weeds by hoeing or removing them with a hand weeder. The grassy weeds — crabgrass, foxtail, barnyard grass, goosegrass, and duckgrass — are more persistent because they spread quickly by runners that go deep underground, making it impossible to pull them completely out of the soil.

Crabgrass, an annual, starts from seed each spring, generally in April, and is at its weakest stage when it first starts to grow. It is important to recognize weeds when they first appear and to undertake immediate control measures or they will gain the upper hand. A good, dense stand of grass is an excellent form of preventing weeds from developing. The *most important precaution* against weeds is a good soil structure with plenty of compost, humus, and leaf mold, allowing quick and vigorous growth of grass. A clay or sandy soil will not provide good growing conditions for

The Persian rug effect, or "tapestry garden" as it was often called in Victorian times, is shown here. The combination of paving and lawn, flowers and walling, all in severe lines, resembles at a distance the carpet effect in color and design.

grass, but it can support weeds, which thrive in inferior situations. Four other successful precautions are:

1. Use a lawn sweeper after midsummer mowings to pick up weed seeds.
2. Aerate the soil as much as possible so that air and moisture get to the bottom of the soil and encourage good grass to grow. Aerate with either a hand aerator or one that attaches to a tiller.
3. Pull up weeds with a trowel or hand weeder when the soil is damp; hoe when the soil is somewhat dry. Cut through the crowns rather than trying to dig up weeds.
4. Cover small areas of weeds with a heavy mulch of building paper or aluminum foil. After several weeks, the weeds' roots and tops will die.

INSECTS, ANIMALS, AND DISEASES

INSECTS. Many kinds of insects attack grass, and you must identify the specific culprit before attacking the bugs with the necessary chemicals (consult your local nursery). When using chemicals:

- Keep chemicals out of children's reach.
- Store chemicals in their original container.
- Avoid spilling the chemicals.
- Set aside a special set of mixing tools.
- Avoid sprays or drifts of chemicals.
- Never smoke or eat while spraying.
- Throw away, but do not burn, empty containers.
- After spraying, wash all equipment.
- After spraying, wash your hands and face with soap.
- Before mixing chemicals, read all labels carefully.

ANIMALS. Moles and gophers can be troublesome and and cause havoc in a lawn as they burrow underground. The ideal solution is to eliminate the grubs and other insects these animals are looking for. But this is not always possible, so you may want to use various old-fashioned remedies, such as mothballs inserted in the tunnels.

DISEASES. Lawns are attacked by a variety of diseases. Grass tends to turn yellow when there is not enough nitrogen in the soil or when the soil contains too much acidity or alkalinity. Brown patch, a fungus disease that attacks all kinds of turf during periods of high humidity, produces irregularly shaped brown patches. Collar spot is also a fungus disease, which attacks Kentucky bluegrass, bent, and St. Augustine grasses. Dollar spot, which causes irregular areas of damage, is prevalent in the spring and fall because of the cool nights and warm humid days. You can control these fungus diseases with a fungicide.

THE LAWN CALENDAR

- *January—March*: Keep foot traffic off the turf to prevent holes and gulleys.
- *March—April*: Fertilize while the grass is dormant, as soon as the snow melts. Lightly rake the area, fill in low spots, and eliminate high spots. Mow the lawn as soon as the ground is free of frost.
- *April—June*: Aerate the lawn and feed it with a complete fertilizer.
- *June—August*: Feed with complete fertilizer.

- *September*: Feed the lawn and reseed bare spots in established turf.
- *October–December*: Apply fungicide before the first snow. Smooth out hollows and valleys.

LIST OF COOL CLIMATE GRASSES

Cool climate grasses are sold as single varieties or in blends. Lawns of a single-grass type, although handsome, can be destroyed by pests, disease, or environmental conditions. A blend of grasses is safer; even if the grass eventually dwindles to only two kinds, it will still yield a green carpet.

Bent grasses.   Bent grasses are fine-leaved and spread by stolons. They need close mowing, feeding, and watering, but do produce a lovely carpet of green. Bent grasses can take either sun or shade. The best bents are Astoria and Highland, which are somewhat tougher than Colonial bent. The creeping bent grasses include several strains—Penncross, Seaside, and Toronto—with fine, flat, narrow, blue-green leaves; they need meticulous care. Suggested areas for bent grass are the Northeast and the East and Northwest coasts.

Bluegrasses.   Bluegrass is considered the best of the cool climate grasses. Kentucky blue is fine-bladed, blue-green, long-lived, and produces a good stand of grass. It needs ample sun. Merion bluegrass is deeper rooted, more intense in color, and more heat resistant. The Windsor strain is a dark, vibrant green; it does well in sun or shade. Flyking Kentucky bluegrass is tough and somewhat more resistant to severe cold and standing water than the others mentioned. Rough bluegrass does well in damp, shady places; it is fine-textured and apple-green in color. Suggested areas for bluegrass are the Northeast, the North Central states, the East Coast, the Midwest, South Central states, and parts of the Southwest and Northwest coasts.

Fescues.   Fescues can endure sun or shade, moist or dry soil, rough treatment, and still thrive, although they cannot tolerate the summer heat of the Deep South. Red fescue and its improved strains—Chewing, Pennlawn, or Rainier—are good for cool climates. Tall fescue and its strains are best for play areas, because they produce dense leaf systems and heavy roots. Suggested areas are the Northeast, North Central states, and the Northwest Coast.

Rye grass.   Rye grass is an inexpensive perennial used in grass mixes. It has a medium-coarse texture, and it is easy to grow in a wide variety of climates, but it does not provide a lush carpet of green. Rye grass is often used as a temporary cover. It takes light shade.

Zoysia grass. Zoysia is a popular grass in the South, although some species are grown in the North. Zoysia produces a low-growing, dark green cover. It takes about two years for Zoysia to crowd out weeds and really become established, but then it is easy to care for. This grass browns off somewhat in cold weather. *Zoysia matrella*, or Manila grass, is fine-leaved and a medium dark green. Emerald Zoysia grows faster than matrella; it has a richer color and is more frost resistant. *Zoysia japonica* and its improved varieties, such as Meyer zoysia, are suggested for northern lawns; they prefer full sun. Suggested areas for zoysia are the Northeast, the North Central and South Central states, the Southeast, and the Gulf, East, and West coasts.

LIST OF HOT CLIMATE GRASSES

St. Augustine grass. St. Augustine grass is effective only in frost-free areas. The variety Bitter Blue makes a coarse, deep green carpet in the shade or the sun. It is available in sod or plug form. Suggested areas are the Southeast and the Gulf Coast.

Bermuda grass. Bermuda grass is the most satisfactory grass for the South. It needs sun, a slightly acid soil, and frequent watering in dry weather. This grass is fine-bladed and spreads well, grows upright, and is a pale to dark green color. It browns out somewhat in winter, but some strains stay green longer than others. Suggested areas are the Southeast, the South Central states, and the Southwest Coast.

Carpet grass. Carpet grass is tall, coarse, broad-leaved, and light green in color. It needs a low-acid soil and grows in the sun or partial shade. Carpet grass is tough to mow. Suggested areas are the Southeast, the South Central states, and the Southwest Coast.

Dichondra. Dichondra is a tough, ground-hugging plant that spreads by surface runners. It has small, bright green, round leaves and grows best in areas with a minimum winter temperature of 25°F. The amount you plant determines how quickly it will cover an area. Plant dichondra early to avoid problems with midsummer heat.

GROUND COVERS

Where climate or rough terrain makes it difficult to establish a lawn, ground covers are invaluable substitutes, because they offer a great deal for little cost and low maintenance. In fact, once ground covers are established, they bind sandy soil, check erosion on hillsides, and quickly cover unsightly

The green lawn that provides the backdrop for this colorful garden of roses and other flowers is almost mandatory: the total effect without it would hardly be attractive. (Photo by C/D Luckhardt.)

There is much Victorian flavor here: arbor, vines, flowers, lawn, and a backdrop of lovely trees. (Photo by Molly Adams.)

areas. Many of these plants grow in shade, and others tolerate full sun and even drought. Ground covers are tough plants.

Evergreen ground covers are attractive all year. There are many plants for mild climates, and there are several for severe climates. In cold-weather areas, start ground covers in the spring. Where winters are moderate, start plants in the spring or fall. In temperate all-year climates, plant them in the fall or winter.

Plants are available in flats of 80 or 100 to a container. Most ground covers need a rich soil; only a few, such as hypericum and vinca, can thrive in poor soil. Most nurseries advise setting plants 12 to 16 inches apart, but this is a matter of choice rather than a rule because the closer together ground covers are set the more rapidly they will cover an area. With 12-to 16-inch spacing, it may take two years for complete coverage.

Shrubby ground covers such as cotoneaster continue to grow for years, and in time they may get out of bounds and grow too high. When this happens, thin them out. Many ground covers become a mass of branches—a solid bed of green—and will not tolerate foot traffic. Others—the flat-growing types—do take foot traffic, but generally it is best to put in stepping-stones if the area is to be walked on frequently.

Every region has its own best ground covers, depending on climate and soil. The plants sold at local nurseries are usually those suitable for your area.

LIST OF GROUND COVERS

Aaron's beard (*Hypericum calcycinum*) grows to 12 inches and takes sun or shade. It tolerates a sandy soil.

Ajuga reptans grows to 6 inches. This hardy perennial has rosettes of dark green leaves and spikes of blue spring flowers. It can take sun or shade and needs ample moisture.

Chamomile (*Anthemis nobilis*) grows from 3 to 5 inches. Here is an overlooked but lovely ground cover, with light green, fernlike leaves. Give chamomile sandy soil, full sun, and even moisture.

Candytuft (*Iberis sempervirens*) grows to 6 inches and is a dense little evergreen with white spring flowers. Give it sun and a rich soil.

Cotoneaster (many varieties) is a shrubby ground cover that has small leaves and decorative berries.

Dichondra carolinensis has small, dark green leaves that form a dense mat. Give these plants a well-drained soil and plenty of water.

Epimedium is semievergreen and grows to 9 inches. It has glossy leaves and dainty flowers. Epimedium needs a moist, slightly acid soil and somewhat shaded conditions.

English ivy (*Hedera helix*) grows in either sun or shade. Some English ivies have tiny leaves, but others have large foliage. A few grow quickly; others take many months to become established.

Heath (*Erica vagans*) grows to 12 inches and has pointed needlelike leaves.

Honeysuckle (*Lonicera japonica* "Halliana") is a tough, rampant-growing vine, climbing to 6 feet. It takes sun or shade and can become a pest unless kept within bounds. Honeysuckle is evergreen in the South, semievergreen in the North.

Ice plant (*Mesembryanthemum*) is part of a large group of annual and perennial succulents. Some, such as Carpobrotus, have 1- to 2-inch stiff leaves; others grow to 8 inches. All have bright, daisylike flowers and need sun.

Juniper (*Juniperus*) is a group of mostly small evergreen shrubs with needlelike leaves; several varieties, such as *J. horizontalis*, are excellent ground cover plants.

Liriope muscari grows to 12 inches and has grassy foliage that forms a dense mat. It takes sun or shade and any kind of soil.

Manzanita (*Arctostaphylos uva-ursi*) grows to 12 inches. This evergreen has small, nodding leaves.

Memorial rose (*Rosa wichuriana*) grows to 16 inches; a trailer and a climber with white or rose flowers.

Mock strawberry (*Duchesnea indica*) has coarsely tough leaves and is a good creeper.

Pachysandra terminalis grows to 5 to 8 inches. This evergreen has whorls of dark green leaves. The plant is slow growing and does not do well in the sun.

Periwinkle (*Vinca minor*) is an excellent, shade-loving evergreen creeper and has dark, glossy leaves and showy white or blue spring flowers.

Plantain lily (Hosta or Funkia). There are many varieties of this plant. Some have large leaves; others have small leaves. Hosta likes moisture, but it can survive a dry situation; it prefers shade.

Rosemary (*Rosmarinus officinalis* "Prostratus") is an evergreen that grows to 24 inches. It has narrow leaves and blue flowers in the spring. Rosemary needs sun but can tolerate a poor soil.

Stonecrop (*Sedum amecamecanum*) is a low-growing succulent that spreads rapidly.

Strawberry (*Fragaria chiloensis*) is a small semievergreen that grows rapidly to 6 inches. It has white flowers and can take sun or shade.

Thyme (*Thymus*) is a low-growing, carpetlike plant that tolerates hot, dry, sunny places and poor soil.

Wild ginger (*Asarum caudatum*) is a handsome woodlike plant for shady and moist areas. It has attractive heart-shaped leaves and is one of the best ground covers.

6.

HERB AND KITCHEN GARDENS

The herb garden was a frequent, handsome addition to the Victorian garden plan, often appearing in formal designs such as knot and sundial patterns. These gardens were generally geometric, retaining pre-Victorian formal design. Today, in contrast, we tend to grow herbs randomly or in borders.

The Victorian herb garden sometimes substituted for the kitchen garden, but usually it occupied a space of its own. In recent years, many such gardens have been reintroduced in small plots. Herbs are excellent for fragrance, flavor, and medicinal uses, so an herb garden is utilitarian as well as handsome.

PLANTING YOUR HERB GARDEN

Whatever the design of your herb garden, find a sunny place for it. Without sun you will have difficulty growing herbs. The site need not be large; some of the most attractive herb gardens I have seen were no more than 15 by 12 feet. Ideally the plot should be near the house, so that you can make quick and easy use of the herbs. But the herb garden can also be an accent feature of the overall garden.

Plant a number of herbs in each bed to emphasize their texture and pattern. Herbs are very colorful plants, ranging from dark green, to gray green, to white green, and many have pretty flowers. Keep color in mind as you plan the garden so that there are interesting harmonies of texture and color.

Once you have found your site for the garden and know what you want to plant, establish paths so you can tend the plants properly and pick them easily. The paths in the formal Victorian herb gardens were part of the total plan, decorative as well as functional. Make the paths of gravel, brick, or even scented ground cover herbs.

The most common herbs are those used for cooking or fragrance: marjoram, oregano, parsley, sage, summer or winter savory, tarragon, thyme, basil, chervil, dill, fennel, and lemon verbena. Judging by the following list of herbs and spices from Charles M'Intosh's *Book of the Garden* (1853) our tastes are not unlike those of the Victorians: "Clove, nutmeg, allspice, rosemary, lavender, parsley, sage, balm, mint, dill, borage, basil, savory, and chamomile."

You can start herbs from seeds in the spring or fall, when the danger of frost is over, or you can buy plants that are ready for the ground and thus save time. Learn which herbs are annuals and which perennials from the list at the close of this chapter.

For seeds, the soil should be crumbly, porous, and have good nutrition. If the soil has been used for years, it is best to spade it, rake it, and add some top soil or humus. This will get the herbs off to a healthy start. Nearly all herbs need a well-drained soil; they will not prosper if roots are constantly wet. Turn the soil to at least 12 to 16 inches in depth and break up any clods. You may want to check the soil's pH to determine whether it is alkaline or acidic—most herbs like neutral soil. Small test kits are sold at nurseries.

After you have prepared the bed, make some shallow scratch lines with a rake, and then lightly press seeds into the tiny furrows. Next, cover the seeds with a scattering of soil. After covering the seed, pat the soil firm with your hand and moisten the area with a mist of water, being careful not to dislodge the seeds.

The germination time for seeds varies from 12 to 14 days for the annuals, for the perennials a little longer. In any case, keep the seed bed evenly moist, never too dry or soggy. When two pairs of leaves have developed on each plant, you can thin them out by removing the smallest ones.

This lovely example of a well-grown herb garden, with all its plants labeled, is a pleasing sight. And what is better than fresh herbs for cooking? (Photo by Matthew Barr.)

LIST OF HERBS

Borage (*Borage officinalis*). This unique perennial has branching stems with gray-green leaves and pretty blue flowers. It needs a slightly poor soil; let the plants dry out between waterings. The leaves have a somewhat cucumberlike flavor and are used mainly for salad seasoning.

Chervil (*Anthriscus cerefolium*). This annual grows to 20 inches and has curled and very finely cut, divided leaves, somewhat like parsley. Plants prefer a poor soil kept somewhat moist but not soggy. Chervil will tolerate some shade if necessary. It can be used like parsley, although it has a slightly aniselike flavor.

Chives (*Allium schoenoprasum*). This perennial grows to 24 inches and has grassy leaves and cloverlike flowers. Chives do best in a fairly rich soil that is kept evenly moist, and the plants are hardy to 30°F. Chives love sun.

Dill (*Anethum graveolens*). Dill is an annual that grows to 40 inches and has finely cut, light green leaves. The plants need full sun and a well-drained soil that is kept moderately moist. Dill leaves can be used fresh or dried; try the seeds in fish and lamb dishes.

Fennel (*Foeniculum species*). A perennial, fennel grows to about 60 inches and thus is not a good choice for small gardens. It has a finely cut leaf and needs full sun and porous, well-drained soil. Both the leaves and seed have an aniselike or licorice flavor and make good seasonings for fish and vegetables.

Lavender (*Lavandula species*). Here is a delightful perennial herb for fragrance; lavender grows to 24 inches and has gray, narrow leaves. Lavender needs full sun and a porous, moist soil that drains perfectly; it is hardy to 0°F. Prune lavender after it blooms to keep the plants compact. Use the flowers in potpourris.

Lovage (*Levisticum officinale*). Lovage is a tall perennial that grows to 50 inches. It needs a moist, slightly alkaline soil and a somewhat sunny location. It is hardy to 5°F. The folliage is deep, glossy green and finely divided. The stalks, seeds, and leaves taste and smell like celery. Lovage is a delightful herb for soups, stews, and salads.

Marjoram (*majorana hortensis*). This tender perennial grows to 2 inches. (It is sometimes grown as an annual.) It has woody stems and small oval leaves. Grow the plant in full sun, and keep the soil evenly moist. Fresh or dried marjoram leaves add zest to any casserole or salad.

Nasturtium (*Tropaeolum majus*). Usually considered a garden flower rather than an herb for culinary use, the perennial nasturtium grows to 15 inches and has lovely green round leaves and bright flowers. Nasturtiums

A small backyard vegetable and herb garden, like this one that has just been planted, is worth its weight in gold, especially in the city. (Photo by Jerry Bagger.)

need good drainage, but that is about all—they grow in poor or good soil, with variable water, in shade or sun. The leaves have a peppery flavor and can be used like watercress in salads. The unripened seed pods are often picked and pickled as substitutes for capers.

Oregano (*Origanum vulgare*). A perennial, oregano grows to 24 inches and has rounded leaves that come to a point. This shrub tends to invade with its underground stems. Oregano needs a well-drained soil and plenty of sun; do not overwater the plants. The plant is hardy to 30°F. Cut back the flowers to encourage more flowers. The leaves taste a little like thyme leaves; use them fresh or dried in Spanish and Italian dishes.

Parsley (*Petroselinum crispum*). A biennial or perennial that grows to 12 inches, parsley has curled foliage and looks pretty in the food garden. It is also a useful plant, loaded with vitamins. Grow it in sun or partial sun and in soil that is kept uniformly moist. It is hardy to 10°F. Parsley can be used fresh or dried with a multitude of foods.

Rosemary (*Rosmarinus officinalis*). Rosemary is a perennial that grows to 48 inches. This favorite herb has narrow and needlelike leaves. Grow rosemary in poor but well-drained soil in a hot, sunny location. It is hardy to 0°F. Use the leaves fresh or dried with chicken, meats, and vegetables. There are both small and large varieties of rosemary.

Sage (*Salvia officinalis*). A perennial that grows to 30 inches, sage has gray-green foliage with a coarse surface. The plant grows well in a poor but well-drained soil and needs full sun. Avoid overwatering, or mildew may result. It is hardy to 20°F. Cut back the stems after blooming to encourage branching. Use the fresh or dried leaves with lamb and meat stuffings.

Savory (*Satureja species*). Growing to 18 inches tall, both the annual and perennial savory have narrow leaves; the annual plant is summer savory (*S. hortensis*), and the winter type is *S. montana*, with somewhat more roundish leaves. Savory likes a sandy, well-drained soil and average moisture, neither too dry nor too wet. It is hardy to 10°F. Keep the stems clipped. Savory leaves have a peppery taste. Use the fresh or dried leaves with meats, fish, and eggs and in salad dressings.

Sweet Basil (*Ocimum basilicum*). This attractive annual herb grows to about 20 inches; it needs a moderately rich soil that is kept evenly moist and loves sun. The leaves have a spicy, clovelike flavor that is good with such foods as cheeses, fish, poultry, and tomatoes.

Tarragon (*Artemisia dracunculus*). This perennial grows 20 inches and has shiny, dark green, slender leaves. Tarragon needs a well-drained, rich garden soil and partial sun. It is hardy to −10°F. The leaves have a tangy anise flavor and can be used dried or fresh in salads, with cheese, and on fish.

Thyme (*Thymus species*). A 12-inch-tall perennial, *T. vulgaris* (common thyme) is the species usually used as a seasoning. It has oval gray-green leaves and needs a light, warm location and excellent drainage. It is hardy to −20°F. The leaves of common thyme can be used dried or fresh in vegetables, poultry, and meats. There are several varieties of thyme, some caraway-scented, others with a lemon aroma.

PLANTING YOUR KITCHEN GARDEN

If we look at old landscape plans of the 1870s and onward, we find that most gardens included an area designated as the "kitchen garden." This is simply another term for a productive garden, one that usually included most of the popular vegetables of today (as well as some with which we are

Herbs and vegetables are convenient to the house in this small backyard garden, a useful and productive area these days. (Photo by Clark.)

The handsome fence is what makes this garden so appealing. Its Victorian character gives the garden the proper definition. (Photo by Molly Adams.)

less familiar, such as salsify), fruits and (later) cut flowers for the home (hence the related term "cutting garden").

No matter what you call it, the producing garden has in the 1980s become popular again. Many small properties include a vegetable and/or a cutting garden, although our reasons are somewhat different from those of Victorian times. The renaissance of the kitchen garden is due largely to two factors: our increased awareness of the vast amounts of pesticide contained in commercial foods, and the runaway inflation that has made many vegetables a luxury; the kitchen garden has become a healthful, money-saving alternative.

So when planning a Victorian garden, try to include a little garden of vegetables. It will prove not only to be a handsome part of the total scene, but a practical one as well.

For convenience, place the kitchen garden near the house. You will be more apt to care for and use the plants if they are close by and in one section.

Find your place for the garden and map it out sketchily before you begin. Plan beans here, beets and carrots there, walls and fences for vining crops (such as squash and peas) somewhere else.

Start with the soil. Any existing soil has generally had the nutrients drained from it, and vegetables really need good nutrition and plenty of water. You can get away with starved soil with some flowers but not with vegetables. Dig down at least a foot, then take the hoe or shovel and break up clods and big pieces. Rototilling is not necessary unless you can afford it. The main prerequisite for good vegetable gardens is porous soil that drains readily and is full of good old-fashioned humus—decayed vegetable matter.

Once you have the site properly prepared, spread topsoil—at least 2 to 6 inches (8 inches is better). When this is done (and it takes work hauling soil to and fro), plant seeds or prestarted plants in rows. Always remember to leave paths so you can get to and from the vegetables.

Put seeds in when it is safe for you to plant in your area; the information on the seed package tells you this. Start cool-growing crops such as spinach in early spring, as soon as it seems likely that the last frost has gone. You can write to the Department of Agriculture in Washington, D.C., for maps that indicate these possible times in your locality. Get your first seed planting in early. If seeds are too much trouble or you do not have time to sow them in early spring, pick up prestarted plants at a nursery and put them in the ground later. It is claimed you get better plants from seeds, but this is hardly true. I used to start all my vegetables and flowers from seed, but when prestarts came in, I decided to try them and found that they saved a great deal of work. The difference is cost—prestarts cost more than seeds.

SOWING SEED.   Once the soil is prepared, you can sow seed, usually in rows. Space vegetable seed according to the directions on seed packets. (It is easy to space large seeds, such as radish and spinach, but small seeds can be tedious.) Label each row so that you know what you are growing. Even the experienced gardener is apt to forget what is where.

The row method gives you space to walk between plants, so you can tend them easily. Row planting also helps you differentiate between weeds and the early seedlings. (And there will always be weeds.)

Before you sow, be sure the soil is moist. The shallow trenches between rows indicate when you have watered enough, because signs of moisture show there. Keep the seed bed evenly moist but never soggy during the crucial time of germination, and remove any weeds that appear, because they take from the soil the nourishment that your plants need.

When the seedlings are 2 to 4 inches high, thin them so there will be ample space for them to grow. This means pulling up smaller seedlings. Discard them, or use them for fill-ins in other areas. Friends are usually delighted to receive extra plants, too.

When you thin plants—no matter how carefully—you are likely to disturb those left in the ground. Therefore, water freely before and after thinning. Not all seeds will come up; some may be sterile, and others may not germinate because of improper conditions. But you will probably have enough seedlings from a standard package to supply your wants.

7.

COMPONENTS OF THE VICTORIAN SCENE

The words *charming* and *nostalgic* are often used to characterize Victorian gardens, but perhaps the ideal word would be *decorative*. Decoration abounded, and nowhere could one find more decorative pieces for the garden than in trelliage.

TRELLISES, FENCES, AND SCREENS

Toward the end of the sixteenth century, the French created highly elaborate structures called *trelliages*, the word denoting a refined architectural use of the trellis. In the eighteenth century, French-inspired trellises were immensely popular in England, often used to form fences or walls.

The old-fashioned summer house was essentially trellis work supporting vines and espaliered fruit trees. As time went on, trellises evolved into arbors or tunnels covered with growth, creating beautiful areas in which to stroll.

It was only natural for the trellises to become part of the Victorian statement, because they were ornate, decorative, and highly patterned, using such patterns as the radial and the sunburst. They blended perfectly

A simple wooden arbor laced with flowering trees and wisteria provides a nostalgic look at the past and makes an ordinary garden extraordinary. (Photo by Matthew Barr.)

with the already overly ornamented Victorian garden and their vertical accent at eye level did much to lighten the landscape.

Both iron and wood were used for trellises, and in many locales, especially San Francisco, elegant trelliage-style iron fences and gates can still be found. Today, however, most trelliage is made of wood, because it is less expensive and easier to handle than metal.

Trellises are handsome on house walls because they soften severe architectural lines and provide colorful accents. Trellis work should not be attached directly to the wall but should be positioned away from the wall so that when it is time to paint the house, the trellis can be laid down carefully with the plants intact.

Handsome trelliage makes this tiny backyard garden an attractive place and provides needed privacy from the street. (Photo by Scharmer.)

For house walls and porch areas, trellis patterns should be simple. Generally, vertical panels supply the most pronounced statements, providing lovely color and eye interest. Wall trellises can also be used around windows and doorways.

Use heavy wood for wall and porch trellises: 1- by 1-inch stock is substantial and lasts for many years. Lathing is too rustic in appearance and too flimsy to use on walls. You can stake trellises into the ground, but it is better to use a frame construction for weight and durability.

Some of the plants the Victorians used for trellises were jasmine, plumbago, ipomeae, convolvulus, celastrus, clematis, passiflora, solandra, thunbergia, bignonia and petrea. Of those plantings then popular, only dinetus, porana, schites, gymnema, tetracera, combretum, amphobus, and momordica are not readily available today.

While the fence may have started as a boundary, it soon became, like everything else in the Victorian garden, an ornamental addition, a work of art. And what better place for floral motifs than in a garden, because many Victorian iron fences were adorned by a graceful leaf curve, a twining stem — the beauty of nature forged by man's hands into decorative additions to the garden.

Some Victorians used fences for the same reasons they used statues — as artistic statements. The union of iron fence with the green of nature not only worked beautifully, it also served to set off the landscape it framed. A well-placed fence is not a barrier but an enhancer of the garden. Transparency and the framing of a view are the virtues of wrought-iron fencing. Implicit in old English wrought-iron patterns, simple and open, was an understanding of these functions. Now as then, a strong, simple pattern with firm lines is best in defining the riot of color and form that is a garden.

Trellis fences and screens achieve the same result. Solid-board fences are not handsome, but a patterned trelliage can produce a dramatic effect. Fence trellises, like almost all trellises, must be constructed with suitable 4-by-4-inch posts and 2-by-4-inch railings as frames onto which the trellis is nailed. A wobbly fence is hardly a worthwhile investment.

Fence designs vary greatly for trellises, but the grid pattern is the best, because it is never too dramatic or too busy. The handsome diamond pattern is frequently used, too. More intricate patterns, with starbursts and sunbursts at the center of the fence, sometimes overburden the design and create too much drama.

A screen or divider area is often needed in the garden or patio to define two separate areas, to create interest, or to guide traffic. A screen can be of any length or height in keeping with the total proportion of the area: wider

The Victorian character is evident in the trellis work framing this attractive patio area. (Photo by Max Eckert.)

and higher screens for large sites and smaller, more intimate screens for small sites. Be sure that one end of the screen fits perpendicularly to the house wall so it looks like part of the total landscape plan rather than as a tacked-on afterthought. Plants do not need to be used on the screen because the screen is really more for decoration than an additional place for growing plants. Generally the trellis screen is painted and serves as "furniture."

Whether making trellis fences or screens, do a rough pencil sketch of the space available. Draw in the shapes of trees, shrubs, planters, and the fence or screen itself. Even the crudest sketch will give you some idea of the mass and volume, balance and proportion, that you are trying to achieve. It is much easier to erase a sketch on paper than to take down a trellis after you build it.

CONSTRUCTION DATA

LATHING.   Building a trellis is relatively simple, because in most cases you are working with lathing. Originally, lath was the thin wooden strip used in lath and plaster. Common outdoor lath was also used years ago for outdoor structures. Today the standard lath is redwood or cedar, about ⅜-inch thick by 1⅝ inches wide. It is sold in lengths of 6, 8, and 10 feet, in bundles of 50 pieces. Usually two grades of lath are milled: one grade has considerable knotholes and blemishes; the other grade is surfaced lath, almost but not totally free of imperfections. Use surfaced lath for your trellises.

Lath can also be made from 1-by-1-inch or 2-by-2-inch wood cut to size. When used in trellis or lattice patterns, lath is more commonly referred to as *wood strips*. These strips are much more expensive than standard lath and must be bought by the piece, not the bundle, but because they are stronger and better looking, they are preferable for such projects as gazebos and arbors.

The third type of lath used for trellises is batten—as in the phrase "board-and-batten." Battens are "overgrown" laths in thicknesses of ¼ to ¾ inch and widths of 1 to 2 inches. Battens can be purchased in lengths up to 20 feet and are sold either by the piece or by the bundle (6 or 8 feet long and 30 pieces to the bundle). Battens are smooth-surfaced and have substantially more strength than lath; they are recommended for more decorative trellises. Battens are about twice as expensive as standard lath but are not as costly as wood strips.

The standard lath in bundles is quite satisfactory for most yard trellises;

it will last two or three years. For more elaborate structures, such as fences and screens, use battens, because they last for many years and always look good. For large structures such as gazebos and archways, use the wooden strips. They look expensive, last years, and make a durable structure.

No matter which type of lath you decide to use, working with it offers a versatile way to make a number of outdoor structures, from the old-fashioned arbor to the more sophisticated pergola. Lath is rather inexpensive, easy to install, and adaptable, and can provide as much or as little cover as you desire.

The most satisfactory lath wood is redwood or red cedar heartwood. These woods resist outdoor conditions because they contain decay-resistant oil and their straight grain makes them less liable to warping. Heat or cold, dryness or dampness will not affect these woods if they are properly installed. If you use pine or fir, apply a coating to them to protect them from the weather.

You can also use tree branches for fashioning your own trellises and arches. This is not easy, but with creativity and perseverance you can make handsome hand-hewed structures. Any durable wood with some flexibility can be used; years ago, larch wood was used for building arbors. If you use tree branches, remove the stems and twigs. Use basketweaving techniques to fasten together larch poles or other woods with strong wire and nylon cord, hemp, or other natural fibers.

Most trellises and lattices are constructed by nailing and epoxying one lath on another lath in a cross or diamond pattern, although heavier wood can be used if desired to increase durability. However, if you have a great deal of wood or if extra strength is needed to support plants, use the interlocking method of building the trellis. For the interlocking construction, follow these nine steps:

1. Use 1-by-1s, 2-by-2s, 2-by-4s.
2. Tape together bundles of 2- by 2-inch strips, 10 pieces to a bundle, with the ends flush.
3. Mark across all pieces with parallel, evenly spaced, 1-inch-wide lines.
4. Tape masking tape lengthwise on your saw to a 1-inch depth for 2-inch strips. Saw down as far as the tape, just inside your markings.
5. With a small hammer, strike between the saw cuts to knock out the chunk of wood, leaving a socket or groove.
6. Insert 1- by 1-inch wood strips crossways into the grooves (they should fit flush).
7. Use 2- by 4-inch lumber for the frame.

Victorian trellis, so very popular in its day, is enjoying a renaissance, and one can see why. It is a charming and attractive adjunct to any garden. (Photo by C/D Luckhart.)

8. Nail strips into grooved pieces.
9. Paint the lattice or leave it natural.

The spacing of laths is important for three reasons: (1) to create a definite pattern, (2) to allow plants to have sufficient room to grasp wood, and (3) for shadow and light patterns. The following spacing data work well for all three aspects. For lath ½-inch thick or less, spacing should be ¾-inch. For lath ½ to 1 inch thick, use a ⅜-inch space. For lath 2-by-2-inches, 1- to 2-inch spacing works well.

No matter what spacing you use, it must be consistent throughout the overall pattern; any variations will be noticed, especially if the lath structure is used for decorative effect, with few or no plants.

The "spacer" can be a wooden block inserted between the laths as you nail them in place. I use a block about 6 to 8 inches long. I lay it flat on top as I nail the lath in place and then again near the bottom when I nail the bottom of the lath in place.

FIGURING AMOUNT REQUIRED.   When you have figured the total area of the lattice work, the size of the laths, and the spacing, you can determine how much lumber you will need. As mentioned, lath is sold in bundles. Thick laths (1-by-1, 1-by-2, or 2-by-2) are sold by the running foot. To determine how much lath to order, use this formula:

1. To determine the number of running feet of lath required per square foot of area, add the width of the lath and the space you plan to leave open between the lath, and divide the total by 12. For example, for 1½ inch lath spaced ½-inch apart, add 1½ and ½ and divide by 12. The answer is 6.
2. To find out how many running feet you need to cover an area, multiply the running feet per square foot by the total number of square feet in the area. If there are 6 running feet of lath per square foot and 50 square feet to cover, you need to order 300 running feet of lath.

For bundled lath, you can determine the number of bundles to buy by figuring the number of running feet per bundle and by dividing this into the number of running feet required. Find the number of running feet per bundle by multiplying the length of the lath times the number of laths in the bundle. For example, a bundle of 50 laths of 6-foot lengths would be 300 running feet.

Trellis structures must be heavy enough to support plants, so framing is absolutely necessary. Two-by-fours provide suitable framing on which to nail lathing. Rather than using very large or long frames, it is always better to make smaller ones; say, a maximum of 4 feet long. The frame is usually made of 2-by-4s nailed together at the corners and further braced with L-shaped braces at each corner. Occasionally a brace—a piece of wood running across the frame—is used for additional support, but if this is done it must become part of the general design.

Once you have made the frames, attach them to something. Some people use an existing fence or whatever is handy, but ideally all trellises should be nailed to substantial posts; 4-by-4 posts are usually the best. Sink the posts into concrete to a depth of 2 feet. Let the concrete set for a day or so; then put the framing and lattice in place. If you build your structures following these principles, they will last years. In essence, trellis making for most structures is the same as basic fence construction: use posts, stringers, and lattice rather than boards nailed in place.

Because redwood turns a lovely silver color after a year or so, most lattices and trellises of redwood can be left to weather. However, if you want a decorative, painted trellis, use 1-inch wood members. It is almost impossible to paint lathing to satisfaction. Even painting 1-inch stock is very difficult.

PATTERNS

There are dozens of patterns for trellises. What you pick depends on your own taste and the surrounding materials and space. Intricate designs — sunbursts or other geometric patterns — can certainly be used and will have dazzling eye appeal, but remember that the more intricate the design, the more time it takes to make the trellis.

If you decide on a special pattern for your trellis work, first make a sketch of what you want. From the sketch, it will be easy to determine how much lumber you will need.

GRID.   The grid is the simplest, easiest-to-make pattern for trellis work and adapts well to almost any garden situation. Nail the lath at top and bottom, horizontally or vertically; then nail the other lath pieces on top, at each end. The open-work pattern allows air to circulate and alternates sun and shade, which is good for all plants. Spacing for the grid pattern is usually 1 inch but can be closer if necessary.

BASKETWEAVE.   The basketweave pattern looks like the grid but the laths are pushed under and over laths to create a basketweave effect. The pattern is handsome but not suitable for all plants because the laths are so close. This is more a decorative trellis than a working one.

STARBURST.   The starburst design is handsome and lends itself well to larger structures, such as entranceways, gazebos, and decorative archways. When you plan the structure, restrict the starburst pattern to, for example, the upper third or the side panels of an entranceway, using more conventional up-and-down lathing to balance the structure. There are several starburst patterns — some horizontal, others vertical — so choose one that strikes your eye.

DIAMOND.   The diamond is a variation of the grid pattern, with diamond-shaped rather than rectangular openings between the lathing. Like the grid pattern, the diamond is easy to make. Spacing is of the utmost importance; keep the spaces absolutely the same throughout the design.

The gazebo, a place of meditation for the early Victorians, adds grace and beauty to larger gardens. (Photo courtesy Rosedown Museum, New Orleans.)

Nail the laths in place at top and bottom, left to right; then nail the other lathing at the top and bottom, from right to left, to form the handsome diamond pattern. Plants grow well on these trellises, and the diamond pattern is fine for fences, house walls, and even as accent panels throughout the patio or terrace.

GEOMETRICAL.   The geometrical pattern is difficult but not impossible to make. The design itself can be of several variations, depending on your own personal tastes. Like the starburst, the geometrical pattern is dramatic and needs a large surface to be at its best. Thus it is ideal for gazebos and archways. Do not use this pattern for fences and house walls because it is too powerful.

ARBORS AND PERGOLAS

Arbors are delightful arched trellises, usually seen overflowing with roses; they are charming in any garden setting. The arbor can replace a gate, provide an overhead structure where plants are grown, or be used as a sun shade. The arbor by itself creates an additional small living area and defines the property.

The design and pattern of the arbor are vitally important; the arbor needs careful attention to proportion and design. A simple grid pattern is not as effective as something more elaborate. You are creating a picture in this structure, so work out the design carefully, and use pleasing proportions.

A pergola is a structure that provides shade by means of plants over a terrace or path. A lovely addition to present-day Victorian gardens, it evokes memories of past days, when leisurely walks were part of the daily life. Pergolas were often concrete or heavy-timbered long corridors, but today we see more of the lattice type, because they are easy to make. Once a crude pole structure, the pergola can now be made in a variety of designs.

The pergola cannot be just tacked onto a garden; it must have a definite purpose: extend the front or the rear walls of a house or delineate a terrace or a secluded section of the garden, for example. The height depends on the space, location, or arrangement of the buildings. Remember, never cut the garden in two with a pergola. It should be a continuation at one end or the other of a terrace or a patio area, or an extension of the house. You can finish one end of the pergola walk with an arbor.

The pergola must be constructed with a strong framework. Proportions should be thought out ahead of time (again, draw sketches). In allowing enough head room for a person to walk underneath, remember that plants may trail downward. It must be wide enough for two people to walk abreast.

Pergola posts should be 3-by-4s, placed at 16-inch centers to support the main framework; 2-by-4s can be used for the transverse beams above. On this framework, nail the trellis pattern. Always put the posts in concrete, because this must be a substantial structure. Lath is the best material for the skeleton of the pergola; finished wood such as ½-by-½ is not necessary, because you want a rustic look rather than a furniture effect.

With the pergola, use decorative vines rather than more utilitarian plants. Wisteria and grapes are perfect, but clematis is equally handsome, and passion flowers and any of the decorative vines mentioned in Chapter 4 are also desirable.

GAZEBOS

Gazebos are Victorian garden accompaniments that are becoming popular as pleasant retreats from the world. They are more difficult to build than anything we have discussed, but as decorative additions to the outdoors they are very appealing.

A gazebo should be located on slightly raised land, since it is intended both as a point from which to overlook the garden and as an accent to it. For these reasons, careful consideration must be paid to material, design, and correlation with the main house.

The application of trelliage to the open structure of the gazebo makes it more decorative and appealing, but it requires some study to work out the right design. Since one is dealing with a four- or six-sided structure with benches around the interior perimeter, one must be careful not to choose a layout too overpowering or overly decorative.

STATUES AND URNS

Until the last century, statuary and urns were an integral part of garden design. This attempt at integrating the human element into the garden was part of the people's love of nature and, more importantly, a statement that man presides over nature. The statues were focal points, reminders to the world that beauty was not only natural but could be improved upon by man and that, while the garden was a product of nature, it still had to be viewed as man's domain.

It must be remembered that great gardens were considered as much an art form as painting, and sculpture, therefore, was thought to have a natural place in the garden landscape.

Statues and urns were commonplace in Victorian gardens. (Photo by Scharmer.)

For that special accent in the garden, a Victorian birdbath is used — urns, statues, and birdbaths were part of the same decorative period. (Photo by Scharmer.)

The Victorian garden borrowed its ideas from the villas of Rome, the allées of Versailles, and the masterpieces of Italian sculpture. While that sculpture itself was no longer a raison d'être of the garden, it remained an important feature. Remember that the Victorians loved to gild the lily. To them a pair of quarreling cupids or a boy on a dolphin served to enhance the landscape.

Birdbaths and sundials of either stone or lead were also part of the Victorian landscape, and urns and vases of all types provided a fillip to nature. The introduction of these pieces into the garden worked well, because it focused the eye on a central feature. When used with discretion, statuary and urns help to make even the smallest garden beautiful.

When adding a man-made touch to your garden, look for classical designs. Urns and pots that duplicate many of the old designs are available through garden supply houses in the United States. Copies of classical statues are obviously more difficult to find, since the craft is disappearing, but they are still available (again through garden supply houses), and many are in good taste.

In all cases, the proper placement of statuary is the key to its success in the garden. Position it at the end of a path, where paths intersect, or in a shaded nook. Place the accent piece at eye level and always position it against a foil—in front of a dark yew hedge or other suitable plant material. Never leave a statue "hanging in air," without the proper background to give it perspective and anchor it to the ground.

TOPIARY AND HEDGES

The grand topiary gardens of France found their way into England in the first part of the eighteenth century, when embellishment in all things, including gardens, was the mode. Along with urns and statues and other architectural details of gardens came topiary—the shaping of shrubs and hedges into animals or figures or even numbers. The ultimate effect of the topiary was to startle or fascinate the visitor.

Today topiary is appearing again, but on a diminished scale. I have seen excellent use made of this technique in large urns, the plants neatly shaped in geometric patterns. Well-manicured hedges, however, are used now much as they were in Victorian times—to establish a barrier, partition, or definition in a garden. The geometric, clipped hedge can also add a desirable note of formal design to a garden. Unlike topiary, the hedge is functional; it blocks the wind and affords privacy without the use of artificial fencing.

PLANTS USED FOR TOPIARY.   Although several shrubs may be used for topiary, the yew is the mainstay of this garden art. It is easily grown in most climates, is long-lasting, can be shaped and clipped easily, and even when cut back severely will return with vigor. The yew can be easily shaped into almost any form with sufficient patience and time. Ilex and box are other examples of plants that can be trained, trimmed, clipped, and pruned. Privet, laurel, beech, and hornbeam are also good for topiary because they grow close, forming dense, easily clipped foliage.

No matter which plant is chosen for topiary, the gardener must have patience. It takes several years before plants are ready for the shears.

104

Splendid examples of topiary are shown here, admittedly difficult to attain but certainly possible on a lesser scale. Yew and boxwood were the topiary materials. (Photo by Scharmer.)

In some parks in America and England, topiary is still used as an attention-getter. One must admit it has a certain charm and beauty and as a novelty is desirable. (Photo by Scharmer.)

Topiary subjects require good soil, proper watering and feeding, and all the essentials of successful garden cultivation as outlined in previous chapters.

Trimming and clipping the plants into geometrical or figure elements is an art in itself. Too much clipping results in a butchered plant and not enough simply does not do the job. Training and trimming topiaries requires ultimate skill. It is very easy for the beginner to rip the foliage and thus create a ragged effect rather than a clean line, which is the ultimate goal.

In the plant's initial years, pruning must be done meticulously and often if the plant is to be trained properly. In the growing season, when the plant is growing fast, frequent pruning is necessary. Suckers (upright, fast-growing shoots) must be removed quickly, and any stray branches must be cut back properly. However, once the final pattern has been reached (several years), it can be maintained almost indefinitely with little change and much less work. Most shrubs and trees produce leaves only on the year's current growth. If the tip of such a twig is pinched or pruned after it has grown a fraction of an inch a new tip develops from a lateral bud on the twig itself but the elongation of the branch and growth of more leaves will be halted. Reducing the number of leaves decreases the plants' capacity for photosynthesis and thus growth.

Use sharp cutting tools for topiary or for hedge work; dull ones only damage the plant. Get several types of cutters—there are many on the market. I myself find the old "X"-type shear an easy implement to use, but there are far more modern clippers available now.

If you have large figures over 3 to 5 feet high, be prepared to balance yourself on a ladder. This is not an easy trick. Pruning from a ladder with tools in the hand requires some doing and know-how.

PLANTS USED FOR HEDGES.   Hedges used effectively are a beautiful part of a landscape design. They can be tall or low, evergreen or deciduous, drooping or rigid, clipped or left natural. They can also be used effectively for tall screenings. Some shrubs trim better than do others; many simply do not respond to trimming and appear shaggy. The best shrub has the desired height, width, and appearance and needs little pruning. Some shrubs are more suitable for hedges than others. They are naturally compact and easily pruned into desired shapes; most are inexpensive. In California, ligustrum is widely used as a hedge.

Because an attractive hedge depends on good proportion, put it in place with care. Do not merely set plants at roughly appointed places and expect an attractive hedge. Stretch a string along the place to be planted and mark a line on the ground. Make the first hole at the end of a furrow and decide how far apart the plants will be. Generally, privet is set 12 inches apart, barberry 12 to 16 inches, and large deciduous and evergreen shrubs about 24 to 36 inches apart; but spacing depends on shrub size.

Evergreen hedges are usually planted in fall or spring; deciduous ones in spring.

Trim hedges wider at the base than at the top to provide for sufficient light for bottom branches. The pyramidal shape is most popular, although other shapes are frequently seen. Evergreens such as yew and arborvitae are sheared either before growth starts in spring or very early summer, or when the new growth has had a chance to harden.

Do not fertilize hedges unless you are prepared to trim them more frequently than normal.

8.

THE GREENHOUSE

The conservatory or greenhouse of Victorian times was dazzling in its ornamentation. The Victorians wanted the beauty of the building to match the beauty of the plants within.

With the importation of so many, often tropical, new plants, conservatories gained in popularity, not only as an adjunct to any large house, but also in connection with smaller urban homes.

Some conservatories were attached to the house itself; others were detached units used mainly on large estates to grow cut flowers for the home or bedding plants for the garden. As the greenhouse gained in popularity, it became somewhat smaller. This smaller form, known as a solarium, was an intimate place, often with leaded windows. Nothing was more gratifying to the Victorian than a vista of brilliant-hued camellias and fuchsias seen down a conservatory walk. Add the trill of a few canaries, so popular at that time, and the result was a bit of nature indoors.

What did the Victorians grow in their conservatories and solariums? Much the same plants we grow today, but favorites were daphne, oleander, wisteria, jasmine, tecoma (once again available), and passiflora.

While the plant inventory remains the same, the design of these glass

A lovely little summerhouse was often included in Victorian gardens, especially when there were acres of land involved. (Photo by author.)

A glass-roofed English solarium, more technically termed a conservatory, was part of many old estates. (Photo by Scharmer.)

gardens has changed considerably. The heavy iron grillwork that typified so many Victorian conservatories has given way to sleek aluminum and, in many cases, wood. Recently, however, there has been a renaissance of the ornate greenhouse, and a few suppliers are starting to handle kit-type greenhouses designed with beauty once again in mind.

VICTORIAN CONSTRUCTION

The Crystal Palace Exhibition of 1851 was housed in a gigantic glass building, an engineering miracle of its time requiring sophisticated methods for glazing and for the erection of steel columns and heavy sash members. Ornate, stately, and endlessly ornamented, it almost single-handedly started the greenhouse revolution in England.

The solarium or orangery, the forerunner of today's greenhouse, was used to nurture flowers and various tropical plants. (Photo by Scharmer.)

The Crystal Palace owed a great deal to the work of John Loudon, an avid proponent of the use of iron over wood. He refuted claims that glass breaks with the contraction and expansion of metal and that iron loses heat by conduction. The alliance of Loudon and his manufacturers produced beautiful curvilinear glass and iron shells in Britain, and domes and quarter-sphere structures promptly mushroomed across the land.

THE CONTEMPORARY GREENHOUSE

In a greenhouse, you can control conditions, so gardening can go on every day of the year. Here you can store bulbs and woody plants, and in February and March, when it is still cold outdoors, you can start seeds and cuttings and save money. The greenhouse offers perfect conditions for propagating your own plants. You can grow vegetables—tomatoes and lettuce from summer into winter—and boxed gardens of herbs under glass. You can enjoy the beauty and goodness of exotic fruits such as figs and mangoes, or enjoy the luxury of cut flowers year round. If you would rather use the greenhouse for a display area—a retreat from the world—you can collect colorful orchids, bromeliads, or lovely begonias.

There is a greenhouse for everyone. You can choose from plastic or glass enclosures with wood or metal framing, in conventional rectangular or lean-to designs, or in hexagonal or circular forms. If you cannot afford the commercially made prefabricated greenhouse kit, you can make your own. An 8- by 8-foot homemade greenhouse cost me $200 and accommodates 100 plants. If this is too much money for your budget, build a greenhouse of salvaged materials. I have seen them built for $50 using old windows and used lumber.

LOCATION.   Years ago there were some stringent rules about the location of the greenhouse: it had to face south or east, run east and west, or north and south. But in fact a greenhouse can occupy any location as long as it gets some sun—a minimum of three hours a day. I had one greenhouse with a southeastern exposure that proved satisfactory; I now have a greenhouse with a western exposure, and this, too, is fine for my plants, although the west sun is hot, so the greenhouse needs shading in the summer. I even have a greenhouse that faces north, and many shade-loving plants thrive there.

More important than exposure, I believe, is making sure that the greenhouse is not under trees that will shade it. The direction of prevailing winds in winter should also be considered. Any greenhouse facing into the wind requires more heat and hence more expensive upkeep than a greenhouse protected from severe storms and winds. However, for all practical purposes, your greenhouse can face east or south, west or north; there will be plants for all exposures, so if you do not have a choice of locations do not let that stop you from building your green palace.

DESIGN.   The most common type of greenhouse is the attached lean-to, the wall of the house providing the fourth wall. There are four reasons for its popularity. First, the lean-to requires little space—an area of 8 feet long and 5½ feet wide is adequate. Second, it can become an extension of the home and a lovely retreat from the world. Third, the lean-to offers easy access in any kind of weather. Fourth, and perhaps most important, the lean-to can be fairly inexpensive. You can buy an 8-by-5½-by-9-foot unit for $189, plus a heater for about $60.

The design of these units is more or less the same: a wall of framed glass or plastic attached at a 45-degree angle to a house wall. The shape varies from straight to rounded eaves, depending on the manufacturer's kit. The frame is wooden or aluminum, and the covering material is glass or plastic. The wood unit looks better but does not last as long as an aluminum greenhouse, which can be used for five to seven years without extensive repair costs. Glass panes are elegant, but acrylic is lightweight, easier to handle, and unbreakable. However, acrylic does turn yellow with time. There are dozens of lean-to's available, sold under various trade names.

Most lean-to's are single-glazed; that is, composed of a single thickness of glass or rigid fiberglass. Fiberglass is inexpensive and unbreakable but hard to clean. Some lean-to's are double-glazed—two pieces of glass with an air space between. Some plastic houses are also double-glazed. This air space greatly helps cut down on heating costs. Double-glazed glass is often referred to as *thermopane.*

The usual lean-to is attached to a ground-level house wall, but lean-to's can also be on a rooftop or wherever there is a wall to which they can be attached. Some lean-to greenhouses are glass-to-ground units; others have a foundation wall that comes about 2 to 3 feet above the soil. To me, the lean-to's with foundation walls always look better. In addition, they are less expensive to heat. The glass-to-ground units are best suited to mild climates.

The lean-to greenhouse varies in size from 5½ feet to 8 or even 12 feet wide (using two lean-to's side by side). The standard lengths run from 6 to 8 feet. There is a greenhouse for practically any area. Because there is such a variety of sizes and materials, it is impossible to list here all the facets of construction of the prefabricated kits. Instead, write for catalogs listed in

Reminiscent of Victorian times, this lovely greenhouse adds charm and beauty to the home and garden. (Photo courtesy Aluminum Greenhouses Inc.)

garden magazines to determine what is best for your own situation. Prices vary from $50 for a small plastic house to thousands of dollars, including very expensive custom-sized and -designed lean-to's.

Detached greenhouses are small-scale versions of the commercial-type greenhouse. The detached unit, generally an A-frame, is usually a hobby area away from the home, a place where you can putter to your heart's content, leave tools out, and let soil sit on the benches without fear of the greenhouse becoming an eyesore when people visit. The disadvantages of the detached greenhouse are that it is difficult to get to in inclement weather, it costs more, and it does not have the esthetic appeal the lean-to has—it looks more commercial. And in the detached A-frame the floor space at the sides is hard to reach. A detached 8- by 8-foot greenhouse retails for about $300 plus the cost of a heater.

This solarium-designed glass garden adjoins the main house, contributing charm and a place for plants. (Photo by Matthew Barr.)

Besides the traditional A-frame, there is a modified A-frame and a gabled-type detached unit especially designed to avoid looking commercial. There are also greenhouses with attractive arched roofs, although these are hard to ventilate.

The detached unit is either glass-to-ground or has foundation walls; what you select depends a great deal on your area's climate. The glass-to-ground unit requires much heat in severe winter climates. The sizes of the detached units vary as much as those of the lean-to's, from 8 by 12 feet to 20 by 60 feet. Greenhouse catalogs list the many sizes available.

VENTILATION.   Ventilation—the circulation of air—is vital for good plant growth. In a closed structure such as a greenhouse, the sun shines on the glass or acrylic, and in a few hours the temperature can rise so high that it cooks plants. Making sure the excess heat escapes is as important as making sure pots for plants have drainage holes so water can escape. Ventilator systems can be ordered with greenhouses and installed easily.

Horizontal ventilators are sometimes used in the ends of the greenhouse; the air is moved through horizontally by electric fans. Another method, and one more often used today, is vertical ventilation. In this system, movable ventilators are attached at high points of the greenhouse roof, and wall ventilators are inserted in the side walls. The air circulates through the wall vents and out the roof vents by convection. Prefabricated greenhouses come with ventilator systems; if you make your own glass garden, you must install these vents or similar systems.

The actual ventilator is no more than a "window" in the roof of the greenhouse. The ventilator can be opened and closed manually by a chain or pulley or controlled automatically by a thermostat that opens and closes the ventilators when the desired temperature is reached. The rope or pulley system of controlling the vents is inexpensive and lasts a lifetime, but it means that someone must always be around to do the job. The automatic electric ventilators have the advantage of working on their own. Especially in the spring and fall, when temperatures fluctuate greatly, automatic ventilators are worth the extra cost—something under $100.

Wall ventilators are usually operated by hand, because they are not used as often as the roof types. You can open them in the late spring and leave them open day and night throughout the summer. In the winter, of course, they should be ajar only slightly so that you do not create drafts.

In the homemade greenhouse, you will have to make your own ventilation devices. Do not attempt to build an automatic system, because it is too difficult. Rather, plan to hinge several glass panes at the top of the greenhouse so you can open and close them at will. Use a chain pulley, which is easy to install and inexpensive to build. Also, remember to install side windows that you can open; do not glaze the windows permanently.

The small greenhouse—the type we are most concerned with here—heats up and cools off rapidly. In a large greenhouse, it is easier to maintain a given temperature because a big greenhouse holds a large volume of air, and temperature changes occur relatively slowly compared with the small greenhouse.

Remember that there are few plants that can thrive without fresh air, and ventilators are the only way to ensure the interchange of fresh air between the greenhouse and the outside. As mentioned, leave the ventilators slightly open, even in cold weather. Good ventilation helps carry off excess moisture and prevents certain diseases. In addition to ventilators, it is a good idea to have a small electric fan in the greenhouse to keep air moving.

You should also have a thermometer in the greenhouse to be sure temperatures are favorable for plants. Buy a good one; cheap ones are useless. Put the thermometer out of the sun and in a place where you can get the most accurate readings, such as on a post where it is shady, or suspended from the edge of a bench. A hygrometer to measure the moisture in the air will help you maintain the right amount of humidity in the greenhouse. Thermometers and hygrometers are sold at hardware stores; there is also a combination thermometer and hygrometer that is quite satisfactory.

HEATING.   Deciding which type of heating unit to buy for the greenhouse is not as intimidating as one might think. However, first consider extending your present home heating system to heat the lean-to greenhouse. This is how I heated my greenhouse; the cost for extending the heat duct was only $60. Consult a heating company (listed in the yellow pages of your phone book) to be sure your present heating system can accommodate the extra heat load. In most cases, it will.

If you do not want to extend your heating system, or if your greenhouse is detached, you will have to buy and install a separate heating system from a greenhouse supplier. The heating system can use hot water, steam, or hot air; the fuel can be natural gas, electricity, or oil. If gas is the fuel, it must be natural gas, because manufactured gas kills plants. Be sure your gas or oil heater is vented in such a way that fumes will be released outside.

Most greenhouses in temperate climates do not have to be heated at all in the spring, summer, and fall. Artificial heat must be controlled only in the winter, and the duration of heating time depends on how severe your winters are. For example, in Chicago artificial heat in the greenhouse is necessary from October 15 until about March 15. A small forced-hot-air furnace with three ducts (about all you will need) will cost no more than $400. A hot-air, gas-fired heater has a safety pilot and thermostatic controls; you will have to install masonry or metal chimneys for fumes to be released outside.

A hot-air, oil-fired heater is small enough to fit under a greenhouse bench. It has a gun-type burner, a blower, a two-stage fuel pump, and full controls. This heater requires a masonry chimney or a metal smokestack above the roof.

Electric heaters are automatic and have a circulating fan but they require heavy-duty electrical lines and are costly to operate. All heaters and devices should be installed by a professional in accordance with local building codes.

ELECTRICITY.   In the excitement of installing your greenhouse, you may forget to put in electrical outlets. Yet you will often want to enjoy the greenhouse at night or show it to guests. And electrical outlets are needed for artificial light and heating cables (for growing seedlings) and other

In a greenhouse, one can grow all the plants the Victorians grew, from ferns to lovely tropicals, and the appeal of nature is brought into the home. (Photo by Matthew Barr.)

electrical devices such as a small fan for circulating air, automatic vents, and thermostats.

For lighting in the greenhouse, incandescent lamps are fine, but the lamps must be in porcelain sockets because of the danger of water shorting the circuits. The lamps or bulbs should also be protected from splashing water: cold water on a hot bulb will pop the bulb immediately. Protect lamps with metal shields, sold at hardware stores, or use outdoor lamps, which are designated as PAR lamps.

HUMIDIFIERS.   Insufficient humidity is not much of a problem in the greenhouse, because the more plants you grow the more humidity there is — plants transpire through their foliage. If you have an average greenhouse — say, 8 by 12 feet, with about 100 plants — the humidity will naturally range between 50 and 60 percent, a safe level for most plants. However, in very dry regions with little humidity, a humidifier may be necessary in the greenhouse to maintain the amount of moisture in the air at a safe level. Humidifiers are available from suppliers for about $100 and are usually installed as part of the heating system. For less money, you can buy a small space humidifier in a department store.

MAINTENANCE.   Once constructed, greenhouses need periodic maintenance. They must be kept clean and tidy, because plants can contract diseases from debris or decayed plant parts in which bacteria are lurking. Check the greenhouse several times a year to be sure it is really spotless.

Maintenance also includes checking foundations for any cracks that might have developed. Caught in time, the cracks can be repaired easily with the appropriate compounds (sold at hardware stores). Periodically check glass or acrylic for cracks or broken panes, and replace panes if necessary. Putty for glazing acrylic or glass in sashes becomes brittle and may chip away eventually; if this has happened, immediately replace the putty before moisture seeps into the frames.

Repaint wooden members as soon as you see signs of paint peeling. Once excessive moisture starts in wood, it can travel quickly and wreak havoc. When painting the inside of the greenhouse, clear out all the plants; it is difficult to paint around the plants, and paint fumes may harm them.

Be sure gutters are in good repair so that water drains freely. Make any repairs immediately rather than waiting until total replacement is necessary. Use a tar-based paint that resists the extra moisture present in greenhouse areas.

9.

BASICS
OF
GARDENING

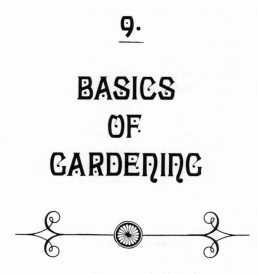

No matter what kind of garden you have, you must take care of it. No beautiful landscape scene develops by itself. Cultivation includes watering, fertilizing, and (perhaps the most important aspect of a good garden) soil care.

CONTROLLING THE ELEMENTS

SOIL.   Earth or soil has two layers: topsoil and subsoil. The subsoil, which has been there for hundreds of years, can begin a few inches below the surface or as much as 20 inches. It varies greatly in composition from sandy to claylike. A very sandy subsoil that retains little moisture is useless to plants, yet claylike subsoil holds water so long that plants literally drown in it. Subsoil should be broken up; in severe cases, a drainage system may have to be installed to carry off water.

Topsoil consists of small particles of disintegrated rock, minerals, and decomposing organic matter. In addition, it has water and living organisms such as bacteria and fungi, which hold the dissolved mineral salts and air. Most soils over the years lose their mineral content, so the soil must be reworked and revitalized. Topsoil may be a few or many inches deep. It is generally a darker color than the deeper subsoil because of its organic content.

There are three kinds of soil: clay (heavy); sandy (light); and loamy (porous). To determine the nature of your soil, crumble a handful. Good soil feels like a well-done baked potato — porous with good texture — and it crumbles easily between the fingers. If you want a more scientific appraisal, soil test kits are available.

A heavy clay soil, one that lumps in your hand, is difficult to work with. It dries out slowly in spring and does not absorb the sun's rays as readily as a lighter soil and thus does not warm up as quickly in the spring as eager new plants demand. Clay soil frequently forms a crust that makes it impossible for air or water to reach the roots of plants. You must add humus and sand to clay to improve its structure. How much of each you use depends on the density of the particular soil.

Sandy soil that falls apart in your hand is easy to work with and warms up quickly in spring, but it does not retain moisture or provide good drainage. And many soluble plant foods are lost through leaching. Adding liberal quantities of organic matter improves a sandy soil.

A fertile soil that is a mixture of clay, sand, and humus is porous in texture and provides good drainage. It is spongy, so it retains moisture; it has humus, so it provides good conditions for the growth of soil bacteria, which is essential for plant nutrition. This kind of soil is good for a garden, but it is rare. In most cases it must be built by a program of soil conditioning.

Humus — animal manure, compost, leafmold, peat moss — is decayed organic matter. It consists of living organisms, or their decayed remains. Humus adds body to light soils and provides aeration for clay soils. It dissolves in the soil and provides nourishment for plants and microorganisms. It is constantly used and depleted and must be replaced. Maintaining the proper proportion of humus in the soil is vital to good plant growth.

A convenient source of humus is peat moss, which is available at nurseries. Although there are differences between the various types of peat available, I have through the years used many kinds, and they all proved satisfactory. A second source of humus is leafmold; it is exactly what it says — decayed leaves and grass clippings. It is easy to make and usually free. Simply rake leaves into a pile and let them decompose.

Another excellent source of humus is compost, and this too is free. Basically, it is decayed vegetable matter of many kinds. Most old-fashioned gardens have compost piles. I would not be without one. It is an easy way to keep improving soil without too much trouble. For the compost pile, select a small (about 6 feet square), inconspicuous place near the garden. Put boards around it to about 4 feet high and leave an opening for a gate. I use 2-by-12-inch boards one on top of the other, anchored in the ground with wooden stakes.

First, throw a few inches of manure into the compost bin and then, as you garden, add grass clippings, leaves, and twigs. Vegetable matter, eggshells, and other similar kitchen garbage can be added to the pile too. When the pile is about 18 inches high, add some more manure and a dusting of lime. Keep the materials moist, never saturated; sprinkle with water occasionally. After a few months, turn the heap, bringing the sides to the top.

There are more sophisticated ways of making a compost heap. Materials can be put through a shredder (from garden suppliers), which speeds up the process considerably. Or you might want to try chemicals that hasten the decaying process. They are available at nurseries under different trade names.

You must be your own judge of how much humus to add to soil. It depends on the soil, the kind of plants being grown, and the existing content of the humus. I mix about 1 inch of compost to about 6 inches of soil; this has proven satisfactory through the years for my garden.

Even though you add humus to the soil, you need fertilizers to supplement it. Fertilizers are not substitutes for humus, nor can decayed organic matter completely do the work of fertilizers. Soil needs both. Fertilizers contain nitrogen, phosphorus, and potassium (potash).

A crumbly, porous soil absorbs water well, so moisture can be transported quickly to the roots of plants, where it is stored for future use. Good drainage is essential, too. Without free circulation of water, its much-needed component oxygen is not distributed to the roots. Waterlogged plants often develop shallow roots and perish from lack of moisture because during dry times they cannot reach down for the stored water below. Poor drainage is a common fault of most soils and is generally caused by a layer of hard earth.

Improve the physical structure of the soil by turning it, keeping it porous, and using composts and mulches throughout the year. Porosity is the key to good soil. Only when pores are in the soil is it worthwhile to fertilize and work your garden. Fertility alone will not give good plant growth—the physical condition or *tilth* of the soil is just as important.

THE pH FACTOR.   The pH scale measures the acidity or alkalinity of soil as a thermometer measures heat. Soil with a pH of 7 is neutral; below 7, the soil is acid, and above 7 it is alkaline.

It is important to know what kind of soil you have, so that fertilizers added to it can be used with maximum efficiency. You can have the pH of your garden tested by the state agricultural authorities or you can run your own test with one of the kits available from suppliers.

Most of our commonly grown trees and shrubs prefer a neutral soil; some grow better in an acid condition, and several types prefer an alkaline soil. Generally, a soil pH as nearly neutral as possible (between 6 and 7) allows you to grow the most plants successfully.

In alkaline soils, potash becomes less and less effective and eventually becomes locked in. In very acid soils, the element aluminum becomes so active that it is toxic to plants. Soil acidity controls many functions. It governs the availability of the food in the soil and determines which bacteria thrive in it. It also affects, to some extent, the rate at which roots can take up moisture and leaves can manufacture food.

To increase the acidity, apply ground sulfur at the rate of 1 pound to 100 square feet. This lowers the pH factor of loam soil about one point. Spread the sulfur on top of the soil and then water the ground well.

To raise the pH of soil ("sweeten" it), add ground limestone (10 pounds per 150 square feet). Scatter the limestone on the soil or mix it well with the top few inches of soil and water. It is best to add ground limestone or hydrated lime in several applications at 6- or 8-week intervals instead of using a lot of it at one time.

WATERING PLANTS.   There are many ways of watering plants— hoses, sprinklers, underground watering systems, and so on. The important questions are when to water and how much to water.

It takes water more time to penetrate soil than one might think. If you water for one hour under normal circumstances, the soil is penetrated to a depth of about 48 inches. So plants that are watered for only five minutes are getting hardly any moisture. Water must penetrate the soil and get to the roots below the surface of the soil. If only the top of the soil is kept wet, roots become too shallow. They do not work their way into deep soil to search out moisture, and they become susceptible to damage from heat.

And I must repeat: although it is essential to water plants thoroughly, it is just as important to *allow them to dry out before watering them again.* If there is too much water in the soil, the supply of oxygen to the roots is blocked, and plants start to drown. Allow enough time between waterings for total moisture absorption by the soil and roots. This is the tricky part of watering—not how much but *how much when.* The *when* depends on wind, temperature, light intensity, humidity, soil, and rainfall. Clay soil holds water longer than sandy soil, of course. And know something about your climate. If you have lived in an area for about a year, you can antici-pate what kinds of winds, temperature, and humidity to expect from season to season.

To offer some guidance about moisture and soil: consider that to thor-oughly soak a 50-square-foot area to a depth of 24 inches, about 60 gallons of water are needed by a sandy soil, about 100 gallons by a loamy soil, and almost 175 gallons by a soil that is heavy or claylike.

A hose under normal volume runs about 5 gallons a minute, so it takes about 15 minutes to soak a sandy soil, 20 minutes for loamy ground, and about 40 minutes for clay soil. The sandy soil will dry out in about 7 to 9 days, the loamy soil in about 14 days, and clay in about 20 days or longer.

An array of watering devices—sprinklers, bubblers, subsoil irrigators, perforated hoses—is available. For average gardens, use a hose or a sprin-kling system—automatic or manual. Sprinklers save time and work, but first you must know how much water they actually give. An empty coffee can will give you the answer. Set it in place on the ground and make note of the time it takes to fill it with one inch of water. Multiply this time by the number of inches you want the water to penetrate a depth and leave the sprinkler on for that length of time.

Sprinkling—from a hose or a sprinkler—is the best way to apply water evenly over a large area. Moreover, many plants benefit from overhead watering: leaves are washed of dust and soot, and the moisture discourages certain pests from attacking the foliage.

A thorough soaking is necessary for all plants, but especially for trees and shrubs. They really need water in growth, so soak them. Put the hose at the base of the water well and let it run moderately for a time, or use a water bubbler that breaks up the force of the flow without decreasing the volume so that soil will not wash out of the well. Another way to get water to the roots of a large shrub or moderate-size tree is with a subsoil irrigator (a perforated pipe that attaches to the end of the hose and is set into the ground).

FERTILIZING. About fifteen elements are necessary to provide nutrition for plants. The three most important, nitrogen, phosphorus, and potassium (potash), are most likely deficient in cultivated soils. In early spring, when plants most need nitrogen, it is generally at its lowest content in the soil—heavy rains may have leached it out. Nitrogen stimulates vegetative development, and it is necessary in the growth of stems and leaves. Phos-phorus is needed in all phases of plant growth, particularly in the production of fruits and seeds; it also produces good root development. Potassium promotes the general vigor of a plant, making it resistant to certain diseases and helping balance other plant nutrients. Also important are various trace elements such as copper, iron, manganese, sulfur, and zinc.

ʃ Plants need feeding when they begin to grow in the spring and while they are actively growing in summer. Generally, woody plants and trees should not be fed after August 1 or you will stimulate growth that may not survive fall frosts.

It is better to apply a weak feeding solution frequently than one massive dose that might burn roots and foliage. Do not feed new plants; wait a few weeks until they have overcome the shock of transplanting. And do not feed ailing plants; they do not have the capacity to absorb additional food.

To feed shrubs, vines, flowers, and vegetables, simply spread fertilizer on the ground around the plant and scratch it lightly into the soil. Water thoroughly to dissolve the fertilizer, which must be in solution for roots to absorb it. Generally, trees are best fed through holes punched in the ground.

Foliar feeding is sometimes used for small plants. Plant food is applied in a solution to the leaves and is instantly available to the plant. Although this stimulates a plant quickly, its benefits do not last long. It is also costly and cannot be relied on for all-season feeding.

Today, there are dozens of plant foods, and selecting the right one can be confusing. Most are composed of nitrogen, phosphorus, and potassium, with some trace elements. The contents are listed on the package or the bottle. The first numeral denotes the percentage of nitrogen, the second of phosphorus, and the third of potassium. These plant foods are called *complete inorganic fertilizers* because they are made of chemicals. However, a 100-pound bag of plant food does not contain 100 pounds of nutrients. The total of the three figures on the bag is what you are actually getting. A bag of 10-10-5 fertilizer has 10 pounds of nitrogen, 10 pounds of phosphorus, and 5 pounds of potash. The rest is inert filler.

Fertilizers are offered in five forms:

- *Powdered.* Good, but blows away on a windy day; may stick to foliage and if stored in a damp place, will cake.
- *Concentrated liquids.* Use for all fertilizing.
- *Concentrated powders.* Dilute in water and apply to foliage and plant roots.
- *Concentrated tablets.* Use mostly for house plants. Dissolve in water and apply in liquid, or put in soil and allow to dissolve gradually with water.
- *Pelleted or granular.* Easy to spread; some granular fertilizers also have insecticides; others have weed killers.

In addition to the man-made fertilizers (most often used), there are nitrogen materials to help plants grow. Water-soluble nitrogen compounds are immediate-acting. Results are quick, but they do not last long, and frequent light applications are necessary to obtain uniform growth over a long period of time. These materials include ammonium sulfate, ammonium nitrate, urea, nitrate of soda, ammonium phosphate, and calcium nitrate.

Slow-releasing nitrogen materials act over relatively long periods. These materials depend on soil bacteria to decompose and transform the compounds into the nitrogen forms that then become available to the plant. There are two groups of slowly available nitrogen materials: (1) organic matter, which includes sewage sludge, animal and vegetable tankage, manures, cottonseed meal, and others; and (2) ureaform compounds, which are synthetic materials made by chemical union of urea and formaldehyde. Do not confuse urea (quickly available nitrogen) with ureaform.

There are also fertilizers for specific plants — for example, roses, azaleas, and camellias. These are specially prepared and are perhaps more valuable for certain plants than are the general fertilizers. It is somewhat like which dog food is the best for your dog.

Because there are so many plant foods, learn which ones will do what for your garden. For example, if you want to feed a lawn, use a high-nitrogen food, such as 20-20-10. For flower beds and to make plants bloom, select a food with high phosphorus content, such as 12-12-12 or 5-10-5. If you want something to improve the soil structure and to release nutrients slowly, choose an organic food such as blood meal or bone meal.

Plant food used wisely greatly aids a plant in producing better growth and flowers. Used with abandon, it can kill a plant.

PRUNING.   Pruning and trimming plants is part of a good garden program. Pruning shapes plants, allows free circulation of air and light, directs growth, and removes dead or injured parts. It also increases the quality or yield of fruits or flowers.

The kind of pruning needed varies at different times in the life of the plant. Many trees and shrubs must be cut back severely at planting time so that there will be strong new growth. Some ornamental trees and most fruit trees must be pruned to grow properly, and of course vines and some trees and shrubs need training to make them handsome.

It is important to know where to make a cut when pruning. Indiscriminate butchering must be avoided. Make a cut only above a bud or a small side branch or a main branch. Do not leave a small stub; it will wither and die and is an invitation to decay and to insects to get into a plant. Cut branches in the direction you want the new growth to take. If you need vertical accent for the garden design, keep the lower branches pruned. However, remove them only after they have served their purpose in nourishing the tree or shrub. If you are trying to shape a plant to a pattern, trim away twiggy and unattractive growth so that well-placed branches can be seen.

Young shade trees need pruning to help them develop strong frameworks that resist wind. Remove unwanted branches before they become formidable. Trim out crossed branches; these give a tree an unkempt appearance. If one branch grows faster than others, prune it when it is young, to keep the tree shapely.

Large trees are best pruned by a professional. Special equipment and skill are necessary when cutting heavy limbs. It is hazardous work, and it is wiser to pay a tree service fee than a hospital bill. Shade trees are usually trimmed in summer, but if the temperature is not too low they can be cut at any time.

In all pruning—but especially with shade trees—never leave a stub. Cut branches flush with the trunk. Cover all cuts with tree wound solution available at nurseries.

Some deciduous shrubs and trees bloom on old branches, while others have flowers on current or new wood. Before pruning them, learn which one belongs to which class. Shrubs that bloom on previous year's wood in spring or early summer can be pruned immediately after they flower. Cut away weak shoots, unattractive branches, and old flowering stems. The idea is to allow light and air to the plant so that new flowering branches can grow. If you prune earlier in the year, thin out only; do not do any drastic cutting.

Shrubs that bloom on current wood are pruned in winter or early spring and will withstand drastic cutting if desired. Thin out weaker shoots to make a more handsome plant.

CONTROLLING PLANT PESTS AND DISEASES

Today's world runs on speed and convenience, and this overflows into our gardening. Yet the very nature of planting and growing things and working with nature calls for patience. When most people see an insect in the garden, they immediately purchase a barrage of chemicals. If they see withered leaves or plants not doing well, they quickly blame insects.

Not all plant problems in the small garden are caused by insects or by disease; sometimes the gardener is the culprit, so look to culture first. Are the plants getting enough water? Are they getting enough light, or too much? What about wind; is it harming a plant?

Leaves with brown or crisp edges may be suffering from too much heat or from fluctuating soil temperatures. New growth that quickly withers may also be caused by these conditions. Lower the temperature, if at all possible, and keep soil evenly moist.

If new leaves are yellow, the cause can be a lack of acid in the soil. If leaves develop brown or silvery streaks, they are getting too much sun. If they appear lifeless, they are not getting enough water.

Buds that suddenly drop off plants are a complaint of many gardeners. This condition is caused by fluctuating temperatures, and there simply is no remedy. If plants are not blooming as they should, they are not getting enough sun. However, if stems turn soft and leaves wilt, the plant is in too much shade with too much moisture.

Once you have decided that an insect is responsible for a plant's failure to grow, identify the pest before buying a preventative. Know what you are fighting before you do battle; and do not think that chemicals will solve all insect problems. Most gardens will still have their share of bugs, good ones and bad, so first ask yourself if an insecticide is really needed.

The small garden will, by its very nature, present small problems. Frequently it is better to use an old-fashioned remedy to eliminate a few insects rather than to haul out a sprayer and mix insecticides. A strong hosing with water rids plants of aphids; beetles can, if necessary, be hand-picked, and mealybugs can be soaked off a plant.

Healthy plants are rarely attacked by predators or prone to disease. They are simply too strong. When you buy new plants, inspect them carefully before you put them in the garden. Be sure there is nothing wrong with them.

In conclusion, if you want to keep plants free of insects, keep the garden clean. This simple step goes a long way in assuring healthy robust plants. Throw away trash, pick faded flowers, cut and burn dead wood.

CHOOSING CONTROL METHODS.   Know how to apply preventatives before you start to use them. There are several methods to control pests. Decide which is the best and most convenient way for you.

Spraying.   Spraying is a satisfactory method because it is possible to reach all parts of the plant. You can use a flit gun or trombone-type sprayer, a sprayer that attaches to a hose, or a portable sprayer. The equipment you choose depends on how much soil you have to cover. Before you spray, be sure the ground is wet. Do the job in early morning or late afternoon; hot sun on treated plants sometimes harms them. After spraying, clean all equipment thoroughly. Wash sprayer with soapy water, rinse with clean water, and force water through the nozzle before you use it again.

Dusting.   Dusting is a messy procedure but it is faster than spraying and eliminates the mixing process. Use a dust gun or crank-type or rotary duster. Do the job on a calm day; otherwise, your lungs will get more insecticide than the plants.

Spreading. The easiest way to eliminate insects is by spreading insecticide. It is fast and clean, and merely requires sprinkling insecticide on the ground and watering it.

Systemic Control. The most popular method of killing insects is systemic control. Sprinkle the poison in granular form (there is also liquid) on the ground, and apply water. The poison is absorbed by the plant roots, and all parts of the plant become toxic to many insects (but not all) for a period of 4 to 6 weeks. The names in this group of chemicals are Di-syston and Meta-systox-R. Although these poisons are popular with gardeners because they are so easy to apply, they are not above suspicion as to their effects on humans. Use them only if absolutely necessary, and then with extreme caution, according to directions on the package. In reality, systemics control only a few insects — aphids, leafhoppers, and mealybugs — and any careful gardener can surely control these without using dubious chemicals.

Biological Control. This method is gaining followers. Biological control is fighting nature with nature and involves using natural enemies of insects rather than poisons. It also includes using plants such as onions that naturally discourage insects. Ladybugs, praying mantises, and lacewing bugs are all part of the organic gardener's weapon force. This control method also involves mulching plants and using a great deal of compost in the soil. It is gardening without poison. It involves not disturbing the balance of nature and, as such, has much to recommend it.

INSECTS. Insects can be divided into sucking and chewing pests. The sucking type get their food by piercing plant tissue, and the chewers bite off and eat portions of the plant. The first group can be controlled with contact poisons applied to their bodies. The other group is controlled by applying poisons to the plant parts attacked; the insects die of internal poisoning.

Some insects attack any plant; others have preferences and limit their diet to specific plants. Although many insects are easily seen, others are so minute they are almost invisible. The most difficult to control, these include root lice, mites, and stem borers, to mention a few.

Timing is important when applying insecticides. Many insects are more vulnerable in the early stages of their lives, after they have hatched from their eggs.

Not all insects are detrimental to plants. On the contrary, many are necessary to maintain a balance of nature. There are many beneficial insects, so when you spray plants to kill aphids you might also be killing the larvae of the lacewing fly, which is a voracious exterminator of plant lice and other insects. Ladybugs, too, eat their weight many times over in insects, and are invaluable in keeping the insect population under control. So are the larvae of the ladybug. Tachina flies make a diet of cutworms and caterpillars. The praying mantis can devour hundreds of insects a day. Digger wasps and wheel bugs are other beneficial insects that eat larvae of various detrimental insects.

Think twice before you start killing insects. There is more involved than meets the eye; many times when you spray to kill a few attacking pests, you may be killing off hundreds of beneficial insects that are, in truth, friends of the garden.

PLANT DISEASES.   Many destructive plant diseases are caused by bacteria, fungi, and viruses. Diseases are generally named for their dominant symptoms (blight, canker, and leaf spot) or for the organism causing disease (rust and powdery mildew). Unfavorable conditions and poor cultural practices often open the way for these agents to cause trouble. A poorly tended plant, like a human being in poor health, is more susceptible to bacteria and viruses. Insects, too, add to the problem, because many of them spread diseases from one plant to another.

Environment also plays a part in the development of bacterial and fungal attacks, because the invaders are responsive to moisture and temperature. Moisture, necessary for the germination of spores of the organisms of disease, is particularly important. Excessive moisture in the soil can lead to root rot. Frequently, plants in shade are more prone to develop disease than those in light.

What follow are simple explanations of the organisms that can cause plant disease.

Fungi.   Fungi are familiar to us because we have seen old bread and fruit on which fungi have developed. There are thousands of different kinds of fungi, some of which can cause serious plant damage. Rot, wilt, rust, and powdery mildew are basically caused by specific fungi.

Bacteria.   These microscopic organisms survive in soil or plant parts and cause blights (including fire blight), rot (including iris rhizome rot), galls, or wilting.

Virus.   Many of the most serious diseases of ornamental plants are caused by viruses. We are still trying to decipher viruses in humans, and they are as much of a mystery when they attack plants.

Listed here are some of the diseases that can occur in plants and the remedies for them. Once plants are infected, it is difficult to save them.

Further, highly poisonous controls are generally necessary, and, although I list some here, I do not recommend their use except as a last resort.

Rust. Leaves and stems are affected with reddish spores in powdery pustules or gelatinous lumps, and foliage turns yellow. Several different kinds of rust affect hollyhock, snapdragon. Spray with Actidione or ferbam.

Powdery Mildew. White or gray growth appears, usually on the surface of leaves or branches of fruit. Leaves are powdery with blotches and sometimes curled. Plants are often stunted. Hosing or heavy rain control it naturally.

Leaf Spot. Leaf spot can do extensive damage to ornamental plants, resulting in defoliation, but it is rarely fatal. Affected leaves have distinct spots with brownish or white centers and dark edges. Cut off affected foliage and spray with zineb or ferbam.

Rot. Many different kinds of rot occur on plants. The disease can attack irises, calla lilies, and other plants—crown rot on delphiniums, for instance. Affected spots appear watery and turn yellow or brown. (The iris borer helps to spread this disease.) Destroy infected plant parts, and sterilize soil before planting again.

Blight. Many different kinds of blights are caused by several kinds of organisms. For example, there are azalea petal blight, camellia flower blight, and botrytis blight. Gray mold appears on plant parts. For botrytis, spray with zineb or ferbam. For other blights, spray with zineb or treat soil with Terracolor.

Wilt. Various organisms cause wilt, which can affect mature plants and seedlings. Usually wilt organisms live in soil. Cut away infected parts. There is no known chemical control.

Mosaic. Mosaic is a virus disease; leaves show a yellow and green mottling and are sometimes deformed. Plants are stunted. Many viruses are distributed by aphids and leaf-hoppers. Destroy infected plants.

Cankers. Lesions on woody stems, with fungi entering through unbroken tissue, are called *cankers*. Cut away infected parts.

Dodder. A parasitic plant, dodder is a leafless vine that suckers to the stem of the host plant. Cut away dodder.

Galls. Enlargements of plant tissue due to fungi, bacteria, or insect attack are called galls. Destroy the plant.

NOTES ON PREVENTATIVES. When you buy insecticides, remember the following cautions. Malathion is safest to humans and pets. Sevin is a carbonate, one of the safest of synthetics. Dibrom is quite toxic. Diazinon is very toxic. Systemics are highly toxic (cumulative and persistent effects not yet fully understood). Do not use metaldehyde, which contains arsenicals.

Check with your local Agricultural Station for further information on insects in your area and suggestions for how to eliminate them.

Insecticides are offered in a bewildering number, and although packages list active ingredients, they are not readily familiar to most people. Many times they are listed by chemical name rather than generic name and they are impossible to decipher. By all means, question your local nurseryman about insecticides. Some are inorganic, others botanical or synthetic. Arsenic is an example of the inorganic type and is generally no longer in use. Pyrethrin and rotenone, derived from plants, are botanical preventatives and are coming back into use. The synthetic chemicals include chlorinated hydrocarbons, carbamates, and organophosphates. DDT is a prime example of the hydrocarbon type; chlordane, lindane, and aldrin are in the same class.

The ecologist's main concern is not how poisonous a chemical is but rather how persistent and cumulative it is. Researchers have discovered that, for many years after application, hydrocarbon chemicals remain in the soil, and that chlorinated hydrocarbons are found today in virtually all living organisms in all corners of the earth. To protect our own world, I feel it prudent not to apply any chemicals that include chlorinated hydrocarbons. The methods of eliminating insects and pests suggested on pages 159–61, although toxic, are not persistent. Surely it is better to have a few plants eaten and a few trees marred than a totally insect-free, beautiful garden with no one around to appreciate it.

Read all instructions carefully before applying chemicals, and always use less rather than more. Handle poisons with care. Keep them out of reach of children and pets. Repeated applications may be necessary. This information is given on the package.

APPENDIX

...

These suggested plans for your Victorian garden are adapted from the book *The Art of Beautifying Suburban Gardens*, by Frank J. Scott, published in 1870. Although I have adapted these plans to today's ideas, the true Victorian flavor of particular arrangements and design remains.

No specific plants have been suggested; rather, I have included placement of shrubs, trees, flower beds, and so forth. Choose your plants from lists in this book according to your region and your personal preferences.

Lots for Victorian homes were usually long and narrow—25 feet by 75 or 100 feet, for example. These drawings, for your convenience, are more typical of today's lot proportions.

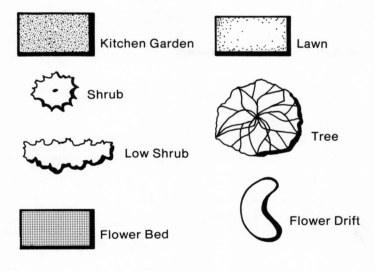

Kitchen Garden

Lawn

Shrub

Tree

Low Shrub

Flower Drift

Flower Bed

Key to Garden Plans

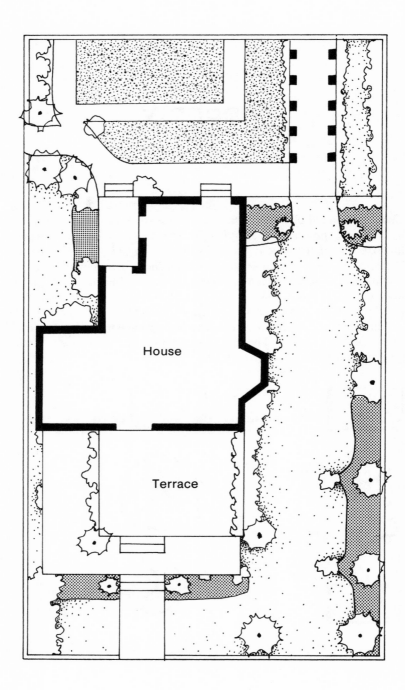

House

Terrace

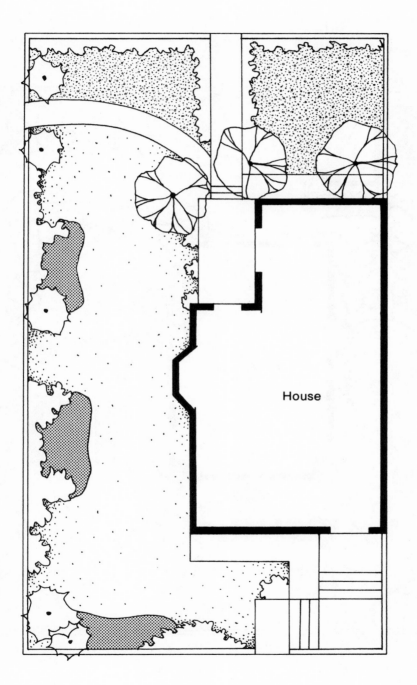

House

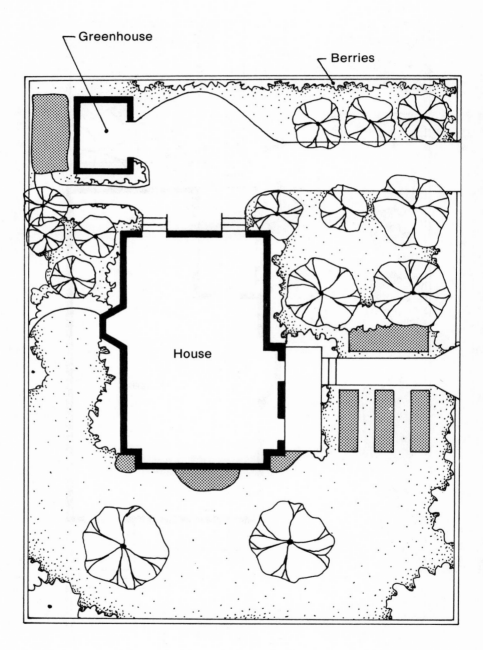

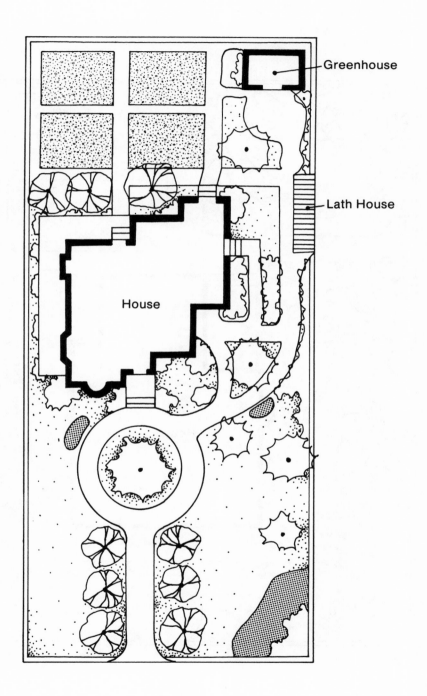

Greenhouse

Lath House

House

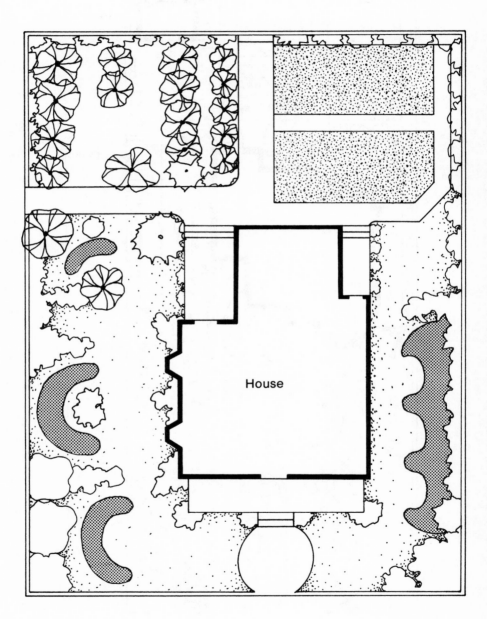

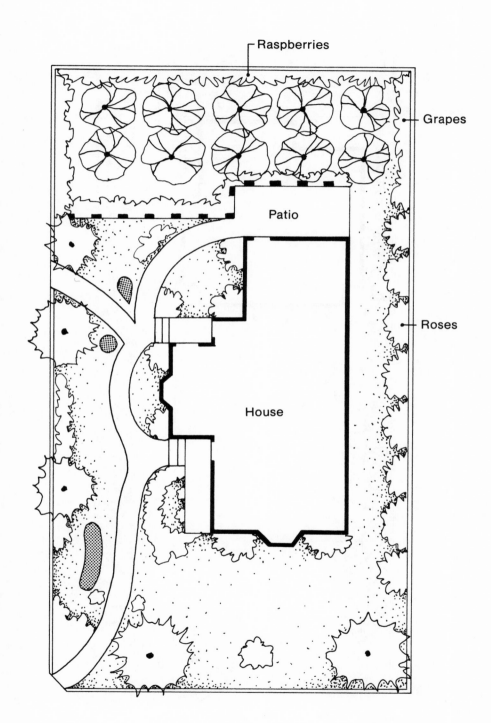

Raspberries

Grapes

Patio

Roses

House

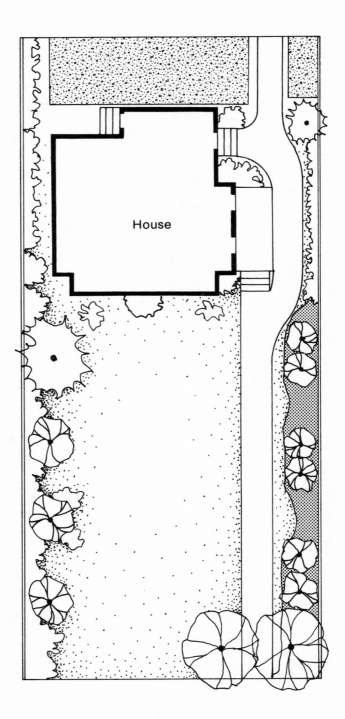

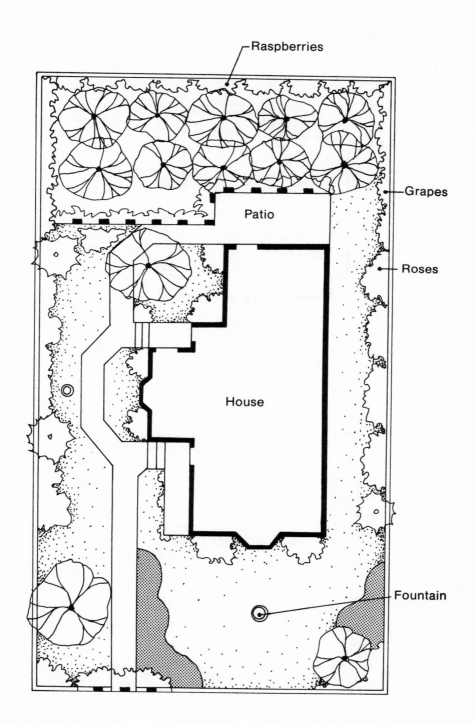

Raspberries

Grapes

Roses

Patio

House

Fountain

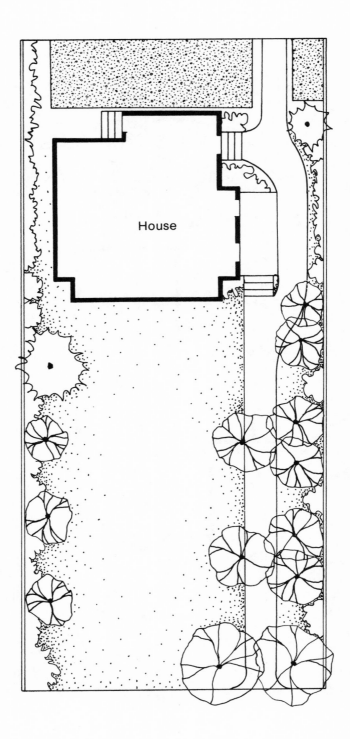

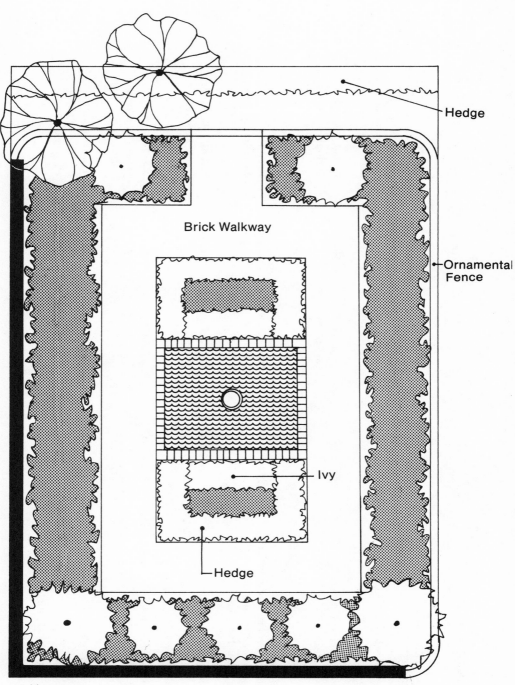

Hedge

Ornamental
Fence

Brick Walkway

Ivy

Hedge

House

145

VINES

Botanical and Common Name	Minimum Night Temperature	General Description	Sun or Shade	Remarks
Akebia quinata (five-leaf akebia)	−20 to −10°F	Vigorous twiner; fragrant, small flowers	Sun or partial shade	Needs support; prune in fall or early spring
Allamanda cathartica	Tender	Dense with heavy stems, lovely tubular flowers	Sun	Prune annually in spring
Ampelopsis breviped-unculata (porcelain ampelopsis) (blueberry climber)	−20 to −10°F	Strong grower with dense leaves	Sun or shade	Prune in early spring
Antigonon leptopus (coral vine)	Tender	Excellent as screen	Sun	Needs light support; prune hard after bloom
Aristolochia durior (Dutchman's pipe)	−20 to −10°F	Big twiner	Sun or shade	Needs sturdy support; prune in spring or summer
Clytosoma Bignonia capreolata (cross vine) (trumpet vine)	−5 to 5°F	Orange flowers	Sun or shade	Thin out weak branches in spring; clings by discs

Plant	Hardiness	Characteristics	Light	Pruning
Celastrus scandens American bittersweet	−50 to −35°F	Light green leaves, red berries	Sun or shade	Prune in early spring before growth starts
Clematis armandi (evergreen clematis)	5 to 10°F	Lovely flowers and foliage; many colors	Sun	Needs support; prune lightly after bloom
Doxantha unguis-cati	10 to 20°F	Dark green leaves, yellow blooms	Sun	Needs no support; prune hard after bloom
Euonymus fortunei (wintercreeper)	−35 to −20°F	Shiny, leathery leaves; orange berries in fall	Sun or Shade	Needs support; prune in early spring
Fatshedera lizei	20 to 30°F	Grown for handsome foliage	Shade	No pruning needed
Ficus pumila (repens) (creeping fig)	20 to 30°F	Small heart-shaped leaves	Partial shade	Thin plant in late fall or early spring
Gelsemium sempervirens (Carolina jessamine)	Tender	Fragrant yellow flowers	Sun or partial shade	Needs support, thin plant immediately after bloom
Hedera helix (English ivy)	−10 to −5°F	Scalloped, neat leaves; many varieties	Shade	Prune and thin in early spring

Botanical and Common Name	Minimum Night Temperature	General Description	Sun or Shade	Remarks
Hydrangea petiolaris (climbing hydrangea)	−20 to −10°F	Heads of snowy flowers	Sun or partial shade	Thin and prune in winter or early spring
Ipomoea purpurea (convolvulus) (morning glory)	Tender	Flowers are white, blue, purple, pink, or red	Sun	Bloom until frost
Jasminum nudiflorum	−10 to −5°F	Yellow flowers	Sun or shade	Needs strong support, thin and shape annually after bloom
Jasminum officinale (white jasmine)	5 to 10°F	Showy, dark green leaves and white flowers	Sun or Shade	Provide strong support, thin and shape after bloom
Kadsura japonica (scarlet kadsura)	5 to 10°F	Bright red berries in fall	Sun	Needs support, prune annually in early spring
Lonicera caprifolium	−10 to −5°F	White or yellow trumpet flowers	Sun	Prune in fall or spring

Plant	Hardiness	Features	Light	Care
Lonicera hildebrandiana (Burmese honeysuckle)	20 to 30°F	Shiny dark green leaves	Sun or partial shade	Needs support, prune in late fall
Lonicera japonica (Halliana) (Hall's honeysuckle)	−20 to −10°F	Deep green leaves, bronze in fall	Sun or shade	Provide support, prune annually in fall and spring
Mandevilla suaveolens (Chilean jasmine)	20 to 30°F	Heart-shaped leaves and flowers	Sun	Trim and cut back lightly in fall; remove seed pods as they form
Parthenocissus quinquefolia (Virginia creeper)	−35 to −20°F	Scarlet leaves in fall	Sun or shade	Prune in early spring
Passiflora caerulea (passion flower)	5 to 10°F	Spectacular flowers	Sun	Needs support; prune hard annually in fall or early spring
Phaseolus coccineus (scarlet runner bean)	Tender	Bright red flowers	Sun	Renew each spring
Plumbago capensis (plumbago)	20 to 30°F	Blue flowers	Sun	Prune somewhat in spring
Pueraria thunbergiana (kudzu vine)	−5 to 5°F	Purple flowers	Sun or partial shade	Provide sturdy support; cut back hard annually in fall

Botanical and Common Name	Minimum Night Temperature	General Description	Sun or Shade	Remarks
Rosa (rambler rose)	−10 to −5°F	Many varieties	Sun	Needs support; prune out dead wood, shorten long shoots and cut laterals back to two nodes in spring or early summer after bloom
Smilax rotundifolia (horse brier)	−20 to −10°F	Good green foliage	Sun or shade	Prune hard any time; needs no support
Trachelospermum jasminoides (star jasmine)	20 to 30°F	Dark green leaves and small white flowers	Partial shade	Provide heavy heavy support; prune very lightly in fall
Vitis colignetiae (glory grape)	−10 to 5°F	Colorful autumn leaves	Sun or partial shade	Needs sturdy support; prune annually in fall or spring
Wisteria floribunda	−20 to −10°F	Violet-blue flowers	Sun	Provide support; prune annually once mature to shorten long

ANNUALS

branches after bloom or in winter; pinch back branches first year

Botanical and Common Name	Approximate Height (inches)	Planting Distance (inches)	Color Range	Peak Bloom Season	Sun or Shade
Ageratum houstonianum (floss flower)	4–22	12	Blue, pink, white	Summer, fall	Sun or shade
Amaranthus tricolor (Joseph's coat)	12–18	18	Bronzy-green crown; foliage marked cream and red	Summer	Sun
Antirrhinum majus (common snapdragon)	10–48	10–18	Large choice of color and flower form	Late spring and fall; summer where cool	Sun
Begonia semperflorens (wax begonia)	6–18	6–8	White, pink, deep rose	All summer; perennial in temperate climate	Sun or shade
Calendula officinalis (calendula)	12–24	12–15	Cream, yellow, orange, gold	Winter where mild; late spring elsewhere	Sun

Botanical and Common Name	Approximate Height (inches)	Planting Distance (inches)	Color Range	Peak Bloom Season	Sun or Shade
Catharanthus roseus (*Vinca rosea*) (Madagascar periwinkle)	6–24	12	White, pink; some with contrasting eye	Summer until early fall	Sun or shade
Centaurea cyanus (bachelor's button) (cornflower)	12–30	12	Blue, pink, wine, white,	Spring where mild; summer elsewhere	Sun
Coreopsis tinctoria (calliopsis)	8–30	18–24	Yellow, orange, maroon, and splashed bicolors	Late spring to summer; where cool	Sun
Delphinium ajacis (rocket larkspur)	18–60	9	Blue, pink, lavender, rose, salmon, carmine, white	late spring to early summer	Sun
Dianthus species (pinks)	6–30	4–6	Mostly bicolors of white, pink, lavender, purple	Spring, fall; winters where mild	Sun
Helianthus annuus (common garden sunflower)	36–120 or more	3	Yellow, orange, mahogany; or yellow with black centers	Summer	Sun

	Height	Spacing	Color	Bloom	Light
Iberis amara (rocket candytuft)	12–15	12	White	Late spring	Sun
Impatiens balsamina (garden balsam)	8–30	9	White, pink, rose, red	Summer or fall	Light shade, sun where cool
Lathyrus odoratus (sweet pea, winter flowering)	36–72 climber	6	Mixed or separate colors, except yellow, orange, and green	Late winter where mild	Sun
Lobelia erinus (lobelia)	2–6	6–8	Blue, violet, pink, white	Summer	Sun, light shade
Lupinus hartwegi (lupine, annual)	18–36	12–18	Blue, white	Early summer	Sun, light shade
Myosotis sylvatica (forget-me-not)	6–12	6–9	Blue with white eye	Spring, late fall	Light shade or dappled sun
Petunia hybrids	12–24	6–12	All colors except true blue, yellow and orange	Summer and fall	Sun

Botanical and Common Name	Approximate Height (inches)	Planting Distance (inches)	Color Range	Peak Bloom Season	Sun or Shade
Reseda odorata (common mignonette)	8–18	12	Greenish-brown clusters	Late spring to fall	Sun
Tagetes patula (hybrids and species) (French marigold)	6–18	9	Same as African types; also russet, mahogany, and bicolors	Early summer	Sun
Tithonia rotundifolia (Mexican sunflower)	72–100	30	Orange	Summer	Sun
Tropaeolum majus (garden nasturtium)	12–18	12–15*	White, pink crimson, orange, maroon, yellow	Spring and fall; summer where cool	Sun or Sun or shade
Viola tricolor hortensis (pansy)	6–8	9	"Faces" in white, yellow, purple, rose, mahogany, violet, apricot	Spring and fall; winter where mild	Sun, light shade
Zinnia elegans (small-flowered zinnia)	8–36	9	Red, orange, yellow, purple, lavender, pink, white	Summer	Sun

* Some spread vigorously.

PERENNIALS

Anemone pulsatilla (prairie windflower) (pasque flower)	9–15	Lavender to violet	Spring	Sun or light shade
Aquilegia alpina (dwarf columbine)	to 12	Blue	Early summer	Sun or light shade
Bellis perennis (English daisy)	3–6	White, pink, rose	Spring, winter in mild climates	Sun
Campanula persicifolia (bellflower)	8–10	Blue	Summer	Sun
Centaurea gymnocarpa (dusty miller)	18–24	Velvety white leaves; purple flowers	Summer	Sun
Convallaria majalis (lily-of-the-valley)	9–12	White, pink	Spring, early summer	Light to medium shade
Coreopsis grandiflora (tickseed)	24–36	Golden yellow	Summer	Sun
Felicia amelloides (blue Marguerite)	24–36	Blue	Spring, summer	Sun
Geum chiloense (*G. coccineum*) (geum)	24–36	Yellow, red-orange	Early summer	Light shade

Botanical and Common Name	Approximate Height (inches)	Color Range	Peak Bloom Season	Sun or Shade
Helenium (various) (sneezeweed)	24-48	Orange, yellow, rusty shades	Summer, fall	Sun
Heliopsis (various) (orange sunflower)	36-38	Orange, yellow	Summer, fall	Sun
Hosta plantaginea (fragrant plantain lily)	24-30	White flowers; yellow-green leaves	Late summer	Light shade
Iberis sempervirens (evergreen candytuft)	8-12	White	Early summer	Sun or light shade
Iris cristata (crested iris)	6-8	Lavender, light blue	Spring	Light shade
I. kaempferi (Japanese iris)	40-48	Purple, violet, pink, rose, red, white	Spring, early summer	Sun or light shade
Limonium latifolium (statice) (sea lavender)	24-36	Blue, white, pink	Summer, fall	Sun
Pelargonium domesticum (Lady Washington geranium)	18-48	Many bicolors; white, pink, red, purple	Summer, fall	Sun

Rudbeckia hirta (black-eyed Susan)	36–48	Yellow, pink, orange, white	Summer	Sun
Solidago (various) (goldenrod)	20–36	Yellow	Summer	Sun or light shade
Viola cornuta (many varieties) (tufted viola)	6–8	Purple; newer varieties in many colors	Spring, fall	Light shade

SPRING-FLOWERING BULBS

Botanical and Common Name	When to Plant	Depth (inches)	Sun or Shade	Remarks
Allium (flowering onion)	Fall	3	Sun	Overlooked and very pretty
Crocus	Fall	34	Sun	Old-time favorite
Daffodil (jonquil, narcissus)	Fall	6	Sun	The name daffodil is used for all
Eranthis	Early fall	3	Shade	Very early bloom
Fritillaria	Fall	4	Shade	Lovely
Galanthus (snowdrop)	Fall	3	Shade	Very early bloom

Botanical and Common Name	When to Plant	Depth (inches)	Sun or Shade	Remarks
Leucojum (snowflake)	Fall	3	Shade	Flowers last long
Muscari (grape hyacinth)	Early fall	3	Sun	Easy to grow
Scilla	Fall	2	Sun or light shade	Once established, bloom indefinitely
Tulipa (tulip)	Fall	10	Sun	Need a cool period

SUMMER-FLOWERING BULBS

Botanical and Common Name	When to Plant	Depth (inches)	Sun or Shade	Remarks
Agapanthus (lily-of-the-nile)		1	Sun	New dwarf varieties are available
Begonia (tuberous)		4	Shade	Outstanding
Caladium		4	Shade	Old-time favorite
Canna		2	Sun	Popular in Victorian times
Dahlia		6	Sun	Always desirable
Gladiolus		6	Sun	Another old favorite
Polyanthus tuberosa (tuberose)		1	Sun	Plant after danger of frost

Ranunculus	1	Sun	Lovely color
Tigridia	2–3	Sun	Making a comeback
Zephyranthes	1	Sun or light shade	Plant after danger of frost

COMMON PESTS AND PESTICIDES

Insects	What They Look Like	What They Attack	What They Do	Control
Aphids	Green, black, pink, yellow, or red, soft-bodied insects	Almost all plants	Plants stunted, leaves deformed	Malathion, Rotenone
Beetles (many kinds)	Usually brown or black, wingless	Flowers and vegetables	Eat leaves and flowers	Handpick if possible, or use Sevin
Borers (many kinds)	Caterpillars, grubs	Woody and herbaceous plants	Wilting; holes in stems and branches	Diazinon
Caterpillars (include bagworms, cutworms, cankerworms, tent caterpillars)	Easily recognized	All kinds of plants	Defoliate plants	Rotenone, Diazinon, Malathion

Insects	What They Look Like	What They Attack	What They Do	Control
Chinch bugs	Small black-and-white insects	Mainly lawns	Brown patches	Sevin
Cutworms (generally in soil)	Hairless moth caterpillars	Many plants	Eat leaves	Sevin, Dibrom
Grasshoppers	Familiar insect	Plants, trees	Eat leaves	Sevin
Lacebugs	Small bugs with lacy wings	Azaleas, oaks, birches, hawthorn; other plants	Leaves appear mottled	Malathion
Leafhoppers	Wedge-shaped insects that hop	Many plants	Leaves pale or brown; plants stunted	Malathion
Leaf miners (many kinds: hollyleaf miner, boxwood miner)	Larvae of various insects	Many plants	Leaves spotted, blotched	Systemics, Diazinon
Leaf rollers	Small caterpillars	Deciduous plants; other plants	Leaves roll up	Sevin
Mealybugs	White, cottony insects	Many plants	Plants stunted, don't grow	Sevin, Diazinon

Pest	Description	Plants affected	Symptoms	Control
Mites	Minute sucking insects	Almost all plants	Discolor leaves	Systemics
Nematodes	Microscopic worms	Many plants	Plants stunted, die back	Sterilize soil
Scale	Tiny, hard, oval insects	Many plants	Yellowing or loss of leaves	Diazinon
Snails, slugs (not insects but common pests)	Easily recognized	Many plants	Eat foliage	Metaldehyde
Spittle bugs	Brown, gray, or black insects wrapped in froth	Many plants	Plants and fruit stunted	Malathion
Springtails	Tiny black jumping bugs	Some plants	Leaves pitted	Malathion Sevin
Squash bugs	Dark-brown insects	Few plants	Plants turn black and die	Malathion, sevin
Thrips	Tiny winged insects	Few plants	Leaves become silvery	Malathion
Wireworms	Hard, shiny, coiled worms	Flowers, vegetables	Kill seedlings; work underground	Diazinon

EVERGREEN TREES

Botanical and Common Name	Approximate Height (feet)	Minimum Night Temperature	Remarks
Abies balsamea (balsam fir)	70	−35 to −20F	Handsome ornamental
A. concolor (white fir)	100	−20 to −10F	Good landscape tree
Acacia baileyana (Bailey acacia)	20 to 30	30 to 40F	Profuse yellow flowers
Bauhinia blakeana (orchid tree)	20	30 to 40F	Abundant flowers; partially deciduous
Cedrus atlantica (atlas cedar)	100	−5 to 5F	Nice pyramid
Chamaecyparis obtusa (Hinoki false cypress)	130	−20 to −10F	Broadly pyramidal
C. pisifera (sewara false cypress)	100	−35 to −20F	Many varieties
Cinnamomum camphora (camphor tree)	40	20 to 30F	Dense branching habit
Cryptomeria japonica 'Lobbi'	30 to 50	−5 to 5F	Pyramidal shape
Eriobotrya japonica (loquat)	20	5 to 10F	Needs well-drained soil
Eucalyptus camaldulensis (red gum)	80 to 100	20 to 30F	Fine landscape tree
E. globulus (blue gum)	200	20 to 30F	Good windbreak
E. gunnii (cider gum)	40 to 75	0 to 10F	Shade or screen tree
E. polyanthemos (Silver dollar gum)	20 to 60	10 to 20F	Fine landscape tree
Juniperus virginiana (eastern red cedar)	30 to 50	−50 to −35F	Slow growing
Picea abies (excelsa) (Norway spruce)	75	−50 to −35F	Not for small grounds
Pinus bungeana (lacebark pine)	75	−20 to −10F	Slow-growing tree
P. densiflora (Japanese red pine)	80	−20 to −10F	Flat-top habit
P. nigra (Austrian pine)	90	−20 to −10F	Fast-growing tree
P. parviflora (Japanese white pine)	90	−10 to −5F	Handsome ornamental

Botanical and Common Name	Approximate Height (feet)	Minimum Night Temperature	Remarks
P. ponderosa (ponderosa pine)	150	−10 to −5F	Rapid growth
P. thunbergana (Japanese black pine)	90	−20 to −10F	Dense spreading tree
Podocarpus gracilior (fern pine)	60	30 to 40F	Robust grower
P. macrophyllus (yew pine)	60	5 to 10F	Grows untended
Taxus baccata (English yew)	60	−5 to 5F	Best among yews
T. cuspidata 'Capitata' (Japanese yew)	50	−20 to −10F	Good landscape tree
Thuja occidentalis (American arborvitae)	65	−50 to −35F	Sometimes needles turn brown in winter
Tsuga canadensis (hemlock)	75	−35 to −20F	Many uses; hedges, screens, landscape
T. caroliniana (Carolina hemlock)	75	−20 to −10F	Fine all-purpose evergreen
T. diversifolia (Japanese hemlock)	90	−10 to −5F	Smaller than most hemlocks
Umrellularia californica (California laurel)	75	5 to 10F	Favorite West Coast tree

DECIDUOUS TREES

Botanical and Common Name	Approximate Height (feet)	Minimum Night Temperature	Remarks
Acer circinatum (vine maple)	25	−10 to −5F	Small, compact size
A. ginnala (Amur maple)	20	−50 to −35F	Red fall color
A. palmatum (Japanese maple)	20	−10 to 0F	Needs rich, well-drained soil
A. platanoides (Norway maple)	90	−35 to −20F	Grows rapidly

Botanical and Common Name	Approximate Height (feet)	Minimum Night Temperature	Remarks
A. rubrum (red maple)	120	−35 to −20F	Best show in late spring
A. saccharum (sugar maple)	120	−35 to −20F	Several varieties
A. spicatum (mountain maple)	25	−50 to −35F	Grows in shade
A. tataricum (Tatarian maple)	30	−20 to −10F	Good small tree
Aesculus carnea (red horse chestnut)	60	−35 to −20F	No autumn color
A. glabra (Ohio buckeye)	30	−35 to −20F	Good autumn color
Ailanthus altissima (tree-of-heaven)	60	−20 to −10F	Very adaptable
Albizzia julibrissin (silk tree)	20	5 to 10F	Very ornamental
Alnus glutinosa (black alder)	70	−35 to −20F	Tolerates wet soil
A. incana (common alder)	60	−50 to −35F	Round-headed habit
Betula papyrifera (canoe birch)	90	−50 to −35F	Stellar ornamental
B. pendula (European birch)	60	−40 to −30F	Graceful, but short-lived
B. populifolia (gray birch)	40	−20 to −10F	Yellow color in autumn
Carya glabra (pignut)	120	−20 to −10F	Slow grower
C. ovata (shagbark hickory)	130	−30 to −10F	Narrow upright habit
Castanea mollissima (Chinese chestnut)	60	−20 to −10F	Round-headed, dense tree
Catalpa speciosa (western catalpa)	50	−20 to −10F	Large white flowers
Celtis occidentalis (hackberry)	75	−50 to −35F	Good shade tree
Cercis canadensis (eastern redbud)	25	−20 to −10F	Lovely flowers
Chionanthus virginica (fringe tree)	20	−20 to −10F	Bountiful flowers
Cornus florida (dogwood)	25	−30 to −10F	Stellar ornamental
C. kousa (Japanese dogwood)	20	−10 to −5F	Lovely flowers in June
Cotinus americanus (smoke-tree)	25	−10 to −5F	Outstanding fall color
Crataegus mollis (downy hawthorn)	30	−20 to −10F	Pear-shaped red fruit
C. oxyacantha (English hawthorn)	20	−20 to −10F	Pink to red flowers

C. phaenopyrum (Washington hawthorn)	30	−20 to −10F	Profuse flowers, brilliant autumn color
Diospyros virginiana (persimmon)	40	−10 to − 5F	Round-headed habit
Elaeagnus angustifolia (Russian olive)	20	−50 to −35F	Vigorous; any soil
Fagus grandifolia (American beech)	120	−35 to −20F	Stellar tree
F. sylvatica (European beech)	100	−20 to −10F	Several varieties
Franklinia alatamaha	30	−10 to 0F	Large white flowers; red foliage in autumn
Fraxinus americana (white ash)	120	−35 to −20F	Grows in almost any soil
F. holotricha	35	−10 to − 5F	Fast low-growing shade tree
F. ornus (flowering ash)	35	−10 to 0F	Dense foliage: pretty flowers
Ginkgo biloba (maidenhair tree)	120	−20 to −10F	Popular one
Gleditsia aquatica (water locust)	60	− 5 to 5F	Wants moist place
G. triacanthos (sweet honey locust)	100	−20 to −10F	Several varieties
Jacaranda acutifolia	50	30 to 40F	Blue flowers in summer
Koelreuteria paniculata (golden-rain tree)	30	−10 to − 5F	Magnificent summer bloom
Laburnum watyeri (golden chain tree)	25	−10 to − 5F	Deep yellow flowers
Liquidambar styraciflua (sweet gum)	90	−10 to − 5F	Beautiful symmetry
Liriodendron tulipifera (tulip tree)	100	−20 to −10F	Robust grower
Magnolia soulangiana (saucer magnolia)	25	−10 to − 5F	Many varieties; also evergreens, shrubs
M. stellata (star magnolia)	20	−10 to − 5F	Very ornamental
Malus baccata (Siberian crab apple)	45	−50 to −35F	Lovely flowers and fruit
M. floribunda (Japanese flowering crab apple)	30	−20 to −10F	Handsome foliage and flowers
Phellodendron amurense (cork tree)	50	−35 to −20F	Massive branches; wide open habit
Platanus acerifolia (plane tree)	100	−10 to − 5F	Popular street tree

Botanical and Common Name	Approximate Height (feet)	Minimum Night Temperature	Remarks
P. occidentalis (buttonwood)	100+	−20 to −10F	Heavy frame
Populus alba (white poplar)	90	−35 to −20F	Wide-spreading tree
P. canadensis 'Eugenei' (Carolina poplar)	100	−20 to −10F	Vagrant roots
Prunus amygdalus (almond)	25	−5 to 5F	Handsome pink flowers
P. serotina (black cherry)	100	−20 to −10F	Handsome foliage; many varieties; some evergreen
P. serrulata (Japanese cherry)	25	−10 to 0F	Lower grower; many kinds, some evergreen
P. triloba (flowering almond)	10	−10 to −5F	One of the best; sometimes classed as shrub
Quercus alba (white oak)	80	−20 to −10F	Needs room to grow
Q. coccinea (scarlet oak)	80	−20 to −10F	Brilliant autumn color
Q. palustris (pin oak)	120	−20 to −10F	Beautiful pyramid
Q. rubra (red oak)	80	−35 to −20F	Oval round top tree
Robinia pseudoacacia (black locust)	80	−35 to −20F	Fine, late spring flowers
Salix alba (white willow)	40	−50 to −35F	Good upright willow
S. babylonica (weeping willow)	40	−10 to −5F	Fast grower
Sophora japonica (Japanese pagoda tree)	60	−20 to −10F	Good shade tree
Sorbus aucuparia (mountain ash)	45	−35 to −20F	Red autumn color
Tilia americana (American linden)	90	−50 to −35F	Fragrant white flowers in July
T. cordata (small-leaved linden)	60	−35 to −20F	Dense habit
T. tomentosa (silver linden)	80	−20 to −10F	Beautiful specimen tree
Ulmus americana (American elm)	100	−50 to −35F	Most popular shade tree

SHRUBS

SE = semi-evergreen; D = deciduous; E = evergreen

Botanical and Common Name	SE D E	Approximate Height (feet)	Average Temperature	Remarks
Abelia grandiflora (glossy abelia)	SE	5	−10 to − 5F	Free-flowering
Abeliophyllum deistichum (Korean white forsythia)	D	3 to 4	−10 to − 5F	Prune after bloom
Amelanchier canadensis (shadblow service berry)	D	30	−20 to −10F	Slow grower
Amelanchier grandiflora	D	25	−20 to −10F	Large flowers
Andromeda polifolia (bog rosemary)	E	1 to 2	−50 to −35F	Likes moist locations
Arbutus unedo (strawberry tree)	E	10 to 20	10 to 20F	Does not like alkaline soil
Arctostaphylos uva-ursi (bearberry)	E	1	−50 to −35F	Grows in any soil; excellent ground cover
Arctostaphylos manzanita	E	6 to 20	5 to 10F	Branching habit
Aucuba japonica (aucuba)	E	15	5 to 10F	Good for shady places
Berberis koreana (Korean barberry)	D/E	2 to 20	−10 to − 5F	Good outstanding colors; red berries
Berberis thunbergi (Japanese barberry)	D/E	7	−10 to − 5F	Grows in any soil
Buddleia alternifolia (fountain buddleia)	D	12	−10 to − 5F	Graceful; branching
Buddleia davidii (butterfly bush)	D/SE	15	−10 to − 5F	Many varieties
Buxus microphylla japonica (Japanese boxwood)	E	4	−10 to − 5F	Low and compact
Buxus microphylla koreana (Korean boxwood)	E	6 to 10	−20 to −10F	Hardiest; foliage turns brown in winter
Buxus sempervirens (common boxwood)	E	20	−10 to − 5F	Many varieties
Callistemon citrinus (bottlebrush)	E	25	20 to 30F	Lovely flowers

Botanical and Common Name	SE	Approximate Height (feet)	Average Temperature	Remarks
Calluna vulgaris (heather)	E	15	−20 to −10F	Bright color and foliage
Carissa grandiflora (Natal plum)	E	15	20 to 30F	Spiny, branching
Carpenteria californica (California mock orange)	E	8	5 to 20F	Showy shrub
Ceanothus americanus (New Jersey tea)	E	3	−20 to −10F	For poor soil
Ceanothus ovatus	E	3	−20 to −10F	Upright grower
Ceanothus thyrsiflorus (blue blossom)	E	30	−20 to −10F	Grows in sandy soil
Chaenomeles speciosa (flowering quince)	D	6	−20 to −10F	Lovely flowers
C. superba	D	6	−20 to −10F	Fine hybrid
Clerodendrum trichotomum	E	10	20 to 30F	White flowers
Clethra alnifolia (summer sweet)	D	9	−35 to −20F	Fragrant summer bloom
Cornus alba 'Sibirica' (Siberian dogwood)	D	10	−50 to −35F	Spectacular autumn color
Cornus mas (cornelian cherry)	D	to 18	−20 to −5F	Early blooming
Daphne odora (fragrant daphne)	D/E	4 to 6	5 to 10F	Fragrant
Elaeagnus angustifolia ((Russian olive)	D	20	−50 to −35F	Fragrant flowers
Elaeagnus multiflora (cherry elaeagnus)	D/E	9	−20 to −10F	Bright-red fruit
Elaeagnus pungens (silver-berry)	D/E	12	5 to 10F	Vigorous grower
Enkianthus campanulatus (redvein enkianthus)	D	30	−20 to −10F	Red autumn color
Enkianthus perulatus	D	6	−10 to −5F	Red autumn color
Erica canaliculata (heather)	E	6	20 to 30F	Pink, purple flower
Eugenia uniflora (Surinam cherry)	E	10 to 15	20 to 30F	White, fragrant flowers
Euonymus alata (winged euonymus)	D	9	−35 to −20F	Sturdy; easily grown
Euonymus japonica (evergreen euonymus)	E	15	10 to 20F	Splendid foliage

Name	Type	Height	Hardiness	Notes
Euonymus latifolius	D	20	−10 to − 5F	Vigorous grower
Euonymus sanguineus	D	20	−10 to − 5F	Best deciduous one
Fatsia japonica (Japanese aralia)	E	15	5 to 10F	Handsome foliage
Forsythia intermedia (border forsythia)	D	2 to 9	−20 to − 5F	Deep-yellow flowers
Forsythia ovata (early forsythia)	D	8	−20 to −10F	Earliest to bloom and hardiest
Fothergilla major (large fothergilla)	D	9	−10 to − 5F	Good flowers and autumn color
Fuchsia magellanica (Magellan fuchsia)	D	3	−10 to 5F	Floriferous
Gardenia jasminoides (Cape jasmine)	E	4 to 6	10 to 30F	Fragrant
Gaultheria shallon (salal)	E	5	−10 to − 5F	Sun or shade
Gaultheria veitchiana (veitch wintergreen)	E	3	5 to 10F	White or pink, bell-shaped flowers
Hamamelis mollis (Chinese witch hazel)	D	30	−10 to − 5F	Very fragrant flowers
Hamamelis vernalis (spring witch hazel)	D	10	−10 to − 5F	Early spring blooms
Hibiscus rosa-sinensis (Chinese hibiscus)	E	30	20 to 30F	Stellar flower
Hibiscus syriacus (shrub althaea)	D	15	−10 to − 5F	Many varieties
Hydrangea arborescens 'Grandiflora' (hills-of-snow)	D	3	−20 to −10F	Easy culture
Hypericum densiflorum	D/SE	6	−10 to − 5F	Fine-textured foliage
Hypericum prolificum	D/SE	3	−20 to −10F	Very shrubby
Ilex cornuta (Chinese holly)	E	9	5 to 10F	Bright berries; lustrous foliage
Ilex crenata (Japanese holly)	E	20	− 5 to 5F	Another good holly
Jasminum grandiflorum (Spanish jasmine)	SE/D	10 to 15	20 to 30F	Blooms all summer
Jasminum nudiflorum (winter jasmine)	D	15	−10 to − 5F	Viny shrub; not fragrant
Jasminum officinale (common white jasmine)	SE/D	30	5 to 10F	Tall-growing
Juniperus chinensis 'Pfitzeriana' (Pfitzer juniper)	E	10	−20 to −10F	Popular juniper

169

Botanical and Common Name	SE D E	Approximate Height (feet)	Average Temperature	Remarks
Juniperus communis (common juniper)	E	30	−50 to −35F	Many varieties
Kalmia angustifolia (sheep laurel)	E	3	−50 to −35F	Needs acid soil
Kalmia latifolia (mountain laurel)	E	30	−20 to −10F	Amenable grower
Kerria japonica	D	4 to 6	−20 to −10F	Bright-yellow flowers
Kolkwitzia amabilis (beauty bush)	D	10	−20 to −10F	Has many uses
Lagerstroemia indica (crape myrtle)	D	20	5 to 10F	Popular summer bloom
Laurus nobilis (sweet bay)	E	30	−5 to 5F	Tough plant
Leptospermum scoparium	E	½ to 1½	20 to 30F	Ground cover and shrubs
Ligustrum amurense (Amur privet)	D/E	6 to 30	−35 to −20F	Small spikes of white flowers
Lonicera fragrantissima (winter honeysuckle)	D/E	3 to 15	−10 to −5F	Early fragrant flowers
Lonicera maackii (Amur honeysuckle)	D	15	−15 to −35F	Holds leaves late into fall
Lonicera tatarica (Tatarian honeysuckle)	D	10	−35 to −20F	Small pink flowers in late spring
Mahonia aquifolium (Oregon grape)	SE/E	3 to 5	−10 to −5F	Handsome foliage
Mahonia repens (creeping mahonia)	SE/E	1	−10 to −5F	Small; good ground cover
Nandina domestica (heavenly bamboo)	SE/E	8	5 to 10F	Red berries in winter
Nerium oleander (oleander)	E	15	5 to 20F	Popular flowering shrub; dangerously poisonous juice
Osmanthus heterophyllus (holly osmanthus)	E	18	−5 to 5F	Sun or shade
Phormium tenax (New Zealand flax)	E	15	10 to 20F	Many hybrids
Photinia serrulata (Chinese photinia)	E	30 to 40	5 to 10F	Bright-red berries
Pieris floribunda (mountain andromeda)	E	5	−20 to −10F	Does well in dry soil
Pieris japonica (Japanese andromeda)	E	9	−10 to −5F	Splendid color
Pittosporum tobira (Japanese pittosporum)	E	10	10 to 20F	Fragrant, white flowers

Name	Type	Height	Temperature	Remarks
Poncirus trifoliata (hardy orange)	D	30	− 5 to 5F	Dense growth; attractive foliage
Potentilla fruticosa (cinquefoil)	D	2 to 5	−50 to −35F	Many varieties
Prunus laurocerasus (cherry laurel)	E	5	10 to 10F	Many varieties
Pyracantha coccinea (scarlet firethorn)	E	8 to 10	− 5 to 5F	Many varieties; valued for bright berries
Raphiolepis umbellata (yeddo hawthorn)	E	6	5 to 10F	Sun or partial shade
Ribes sanguineum (flowering currant)	D	4 to 12	−10 to − 5F	Deep-red flowers; March to June
Salix caprea (French pussy willow)	D	25	−20 to −10F	Vigorous grower
Salix repens (creeping willow)	D	3	−20 to −10F	Good low willow for poor soil
Sarcococca ruscifolia	E	6	5 to 10F	Takes shade
Skimmia japonica (Japanese skimmia)	E	4	5 to 10F	For shade
Spiraea arguta	D	6	−20 to −10F	Free-flowering
Spiraea prunifolia (bridal wreath spiraea)	D	9	−20 to −10F	Turns orange in fall
Spiraea thunbergi (thunberg spiraea)	D	5	−20 to −10F	Arching branches
Spiraea veitchii	D	12	−10 to − 5F	Good background; graceful one
Syringa henryi 'Lutece'	D	10	−50 to −35F	Early June bloom
Syringa villosa (late lilac)	D	9	−50 to −35F	Dense, upright habit
Syringa vulgaris (common lilac)	D	20	−35 to −20F	Many varieties
Tamarix aphylla (Athel tree)	E	30 to 50	5 to 10F	Good wide-spread tree
Tamarix parviflora 'Pink Cascade, Summer Glow'	D	15	−20 to −10F	Prune immediately after bloom
Taxus canadensis (Canada yew)	E	3 to 6	−50 to −35F	Will tolerate shade
Viburnum davidi	E	3	5 to 10 F	Handsome leaves
Viburnum dentatum (arrowwood)	D	15	−50 to −35F	Red fall color
Viburnum dilatatum (linden viburnum)	D	9	−10 to − 5F	Colorful red fruit
Viburnum lantana (wayfaring tree)	D	15	−35 to −20F	Grows in dry soil
Viburnum lentago (nannyberry)	D	30	−50 to −35F	Good background or screen plant

Botanical and Common Name	SE D E	Approximate Height (feet)	Average Temperature	Remarks
Viburnum opulus (European cranberry bush)	D	12	−35 to −20F	Many varieties
Viburnum prunifolium (black haw)	D	15	−35 to −20F	Good specimen plant
Viburnum sieboldi	D	30	−20 to −10F	Stellar performer
Viburnum trilobum (cranberry bush)	D	12	−50 to −35F	Effective in winter
Vitex agnus-castus (chaste tree)	D	9	− 5 to 10F	Lilac flowers
Weigela 'Bristol Ruby'	D	7	−10 to − 5F	Complex hybrid
Weigela 'Bristol Snowflake'	D	7	−10 to − 5F	Complex hybrid
Weigela florida	D	9	−10 to − 5F	Many available
Weigela middendorfiana	D	1	−20 to −10F	Dense, broad shrubs

FOR FURTHER READING

...

Clifford, Derek. *A History of Garden Design*. London: Faber & Faber, 1962.

Crowe, Sylvia. *Garden Design*. New York: Hearthside Press, 1952.

Gothein, Marie Luise. *A History of Garden Art*. New York: Hacker Art Books, 1966.

Hyams, Edward. *A History of Gardens and Gardening*. New York: Praeger Publishers, 1971.

———. *The English Garden*. London: Thames and Hudson, 1964.

Kramer, Jack. *The Old Fashioned Cutting Garden*. New York: Macmillan, 1979.

Loudon, J. C. *An Encyclopedia of Gardening*. London, 1822.

———. *The Suburban Garden and Villa Companion*. London, 1832.

M'Intosh, Charles. *The Book of the Garden*. 2 vols. London: William Blackwood and Sons, 1853.

Nichols, Rose Standish. *English Pleasure Gardens*. London: Macmillan, 1902.

Nuese, Josephine. *The Country Garden*. New York: Charles Scribner's Sons, 1970.

Ortloff, H. Stuart, and Raymore, Henry B. *The Book of Landscape Design*. New York: M. Barrows, 1959.

Repton, Humphrey. *Observations on the Theory and Practice of Landscape Gardening*. London, 1803.

———. *Sketches of Hints on Landscape Gardening*. London, 1795.

Richey, Elinor. *The Ultimate Victorians*. Berkeley, Calif.: Howell-North Books, 1970.

Victorian Landscape Gardening: A Facsimile of Jacob Weidenmann's "Beautifying Country Homes." Watkins Glen, N.Y.: American Life Foundation, 1978.

INDEX